PYTHON

FOR
ABSOLUTE BEGINNERS

A Step-by-Step Guide to Learn Python Programming from
Scratch, with Practical Coding Examples and Exercises

ANDREW WARNER

DEDICATION

To my loving wife, Rachael

Whenever I look into your eyes, I feel the same way as I felt on the day we first met and I looked into your eyes.

CONTENTS

INTRODUCTION

C omputers have become part and parcel of everyone's life. No matter where you are in the world or what lifestyle you have, you interact with at least one every day. From the watch you wear to the blender in your kitchen, they make a difference in how you live. And with 5G and smart devices set to become mainstream in the near future, you must be tech-savvy just to go about your day.
Simply put, a computer is a machine that has a set of instructions — a.k.a. program or software — to do a specific task(s). Without codes, it is just a piece of junk hardware. The people who write them are called programmers, software developers, or coders. The medium they use to write these instructions is known as a programming language.

Thanks to rapid technological advancements, the computer already gives a high degree of freedom to programmers. You have storage devices in gigabytes and even terabytes now instead of just a few kilobytes that were mostly available 30 years ago. Its processing power has increased tremendously as well. Computers are amazing at repetitive jobs that people cannot do. They lack emotions that tend to cause human error.

All these things have led to the invention of high-level programming languages. They have enabled programmers to develop complex software solutions that can tackle virtually any task. This has resulted in automation becoming a part of everyone's personal and professional lives.

This book is written for programming enthusiasts who want to learn how to do it from scratch. Even though modern programming languages don't have many of them, it's a good idea to understand the limitations and the basic concepts before learning a specific language. Also, every field has its own terminology. If you don't familiarize yourself with it from the start, you may feel challenged when you move to advanced concepts.

Modern programming languages are very condensed. What required 100 lines of code in an older language, for instance, might need 5 lines of codes only using a modern one. You'll notice later that the codes here are as simple as possible even if it takes a little more line to achieve the goal. There are also programming techniques available in every language for shortcuts and code optimization.

Nevertheless, that is not the main purpose of this book. The goal is to impart basic concepts of programming and help you learn Python.

Why Python, you may ask?

Well, for starters, Python is as effective as a learning language as it is in tackling complex tasks. It is one of the easiest high-level modern programming languages to learn. The syntax is fairly easy to get accustomed to; it's powerful and integrates with other programming languages and systems nicely. On top of that, its capabilities are highly extendible, thanks to dozens of libraries and external modules. After you have learned programming and Python concepts within this book, you don't need to switch to another language in the future to pursue further skills.

PYTHON FOR ABSOLUTE BEGINNERS

CHAPTER ONE

PROGRAMMING BASICS

A ll programming languages have the same concepts at the core. Over the years, though, they have evolved to offer more power and relieve coders from worrying about minute details.

The first programming language I learned was Basic in school. The only thing I got from it was printing my name ten times on the screen, but that software intrigued me enough to pursue programming as a profession. The problem was, I made the mistake of learning a language without knowing its underlying concepts. It was fine at first, but as I started to explore advanced ideas, they became almost impossible to understand.

To help you avoid the same issue, we will discuss the basic concepts in this chapter.

Integral Programming Concepts

It is important to understand how programming languages differ.

Some of them are suitable for text processing, graphics, mathematical applications, or general purposes.

There is no standard classification system for programming languages. It depends on the criteria you use to classify them. Here is a simplified version of that:

Low-Level Languages

During the early 20th century, computers had limited resources. It was the programmer's duty to keep track of resource usage when writing a program. Computers also had limited capabilities as they only understood a small set of instructions. These are some of the reasons why low-level languages came into existence.

Machine Language

This is the only language that computers understand because it comprises the binary codes that computer hardware uses. During the machine language era, programming was not even a distinct field. There were no standards, and writing programs was a nightmare. Have you seen Margaret Hamilton's picture along with the software that she wrote for the Apollo program that helped a man land on the moon? If not, do it and read her story. You'll understand what I am trying to say. Later on, programmers were able to use hexadecimal codes. Still, the entire process was very complicated.

As a demonstration of how complex and lengthy the coding process was in machine language, here's the binary code conversion of the two-word phrase "Hello universe!"

```
01001000   01100101   01101100   01101100   01101111   00100000
01110101   01101110   01101001   01110110   01100101   01110010
01110011   01100101
```

Assembly Language

Assembly languages were the first ones to pave the way for problem solving using computers on a commercial scale. Long binary codes were replaced with short alphanumeric codes that were easier to input and store. Digital input devices like keyboard became mainstream, so punch cards ended up being obsolete.

High-Level Languages

All modern programming languages are high-level. They give you freedom from hardware considerations to execute a program. Programmers focus on achieving results while the programming platform does the resource management, which is not required in most cases due to the advanced computer systems that we have nowadays.

Problem-Oriented Language

Programming languages like Java, Perl, and Python are problem-oriented. They enable programmers to focus on solving the task at hand and forget about the hardware resources. It's all about the final product. coding has become easier and there are so many resources available that you don't need to do everything from scratch. You can pick ready-made modules and repurpose them to fit your requirements.

Natural Programming Language

We already have devices that process human languages on a limited scale and even detect different voices and accents. Further progress is happening rapidly in the field of artificial intelligence (AI) with the objective of giving human-level intellect and freedom of choice to computers and enabling them to make independent decisions. At the heart of this are the natural programming languages that'll allow devices to seamlessly understand human language. Have you seen a science-fiction movie about a human-like robot who lives and participates in the society like the rest of us? This is where we are headed.

Interpreters and Compilers

In all high-level languages, the programs are either interpreted or compiled for the computer to understand what needs to be done.

In interpreters, each line of code is translated to machine language and executed as soon as it's entered. Interpreter languages are useful for testing and learning. An example of such language is Ruby.

In compilers, the entire program is converted to machine language called object code and saved for future executions. If the original program isn't changed, compiler ignores the conversion step and executes the object code, which makes the process faster. This technique is good for large software that strain available resources. An example of this language is C.

Python is basically an interpreter language but also offers compiler option for large programs. It highlights the versatility of the language once again.

Important Definitions

Syntax

Syntax is the set of rules that governs how to write code in a programming language. Just like real-life languages, it's essential to follow the specific syntax to avoid unexpected results.

Algorithms

Writing algorithms is an age-old method of solving problems in a step-by-step way. It is loosely based on the approach that mathematicians have used to formulate theorems for centuries. Every professional programmer writes an algorithm before writing a program to solve an issue. Here's a simple algorithm to make yourself a cheese omelet:

1. Wake up at 7am.
2. Check if you have all the ingredients. If not, go to the corner store and buy the missing ones.

3. Cut the vegetables, whisk the eggs, and mix all the ingredients in it except oil.
4. Heat very little oil in the non-stick pan and add the batter.
5. Once one side is done, flip and add a cheese slice.
6. Flip the egg once again after cheese is melted and cook to set.
7. Enjoy it with bread or as is.

Flowcharts

As the name suggests, it is a method to record the flow of a solution. It's a bit technical and makes more sense to programmers because different boxes indicate various programming techniques. For example, if the next step in the program flow is to check a condition that can lead to two different scenarios, the symbol below is used.

Here is the flowchart for the algorithm I wrote for making cheese omelet:

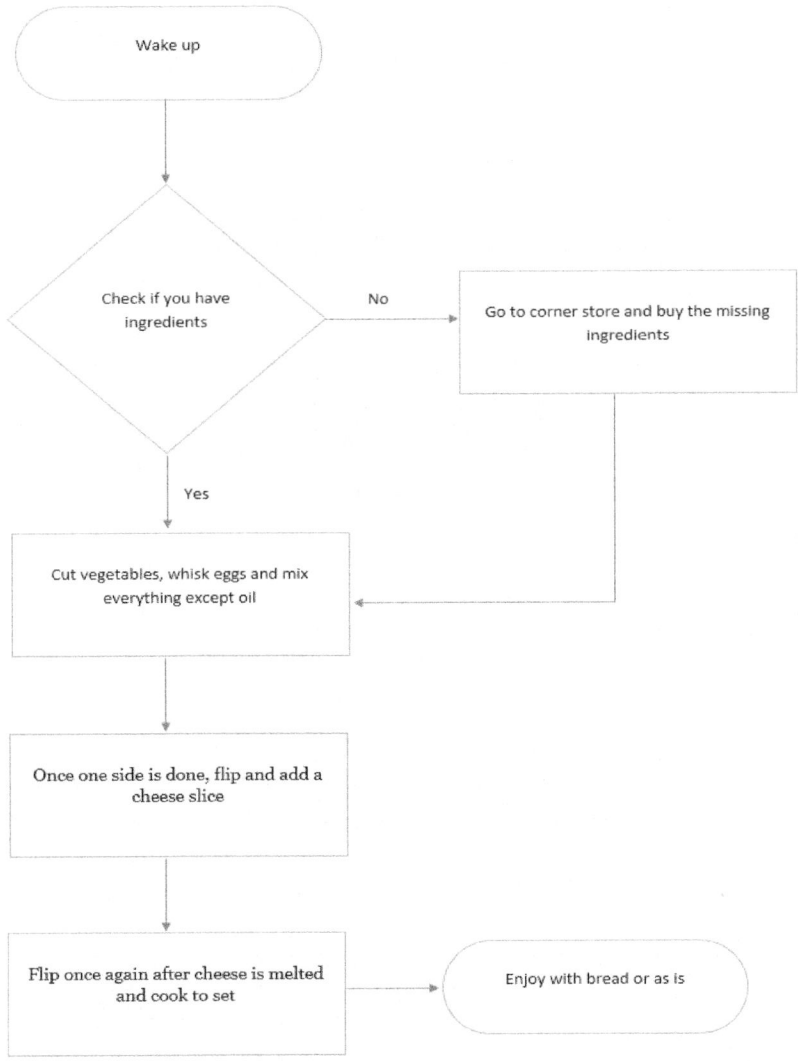

Flow of Execution

Also referred to as control flow, this determines how a programming language executes a piece of code. For example, Python executes one line of code from top to bottom. The flow can be changed using a loop or conditions. We'll discuss this in detail in Chapter 3.

Keywords

Every programming language has some words that have special meaning. You cannot use these words apart from the purpose they have in that specific language. In short, their usage is reserved.

Mathematics

Mathematics is the branch of science that basically has no set definition. It is a broad field that deals with the study of quantity (arithmetic), structure (algebra), space (trigonometry), and change (calculus) to reach solution of known problems. If you are weak in mathematics, you may struggle with programming. Many related techniques and concepts, after all, have been borrowed straight from this field.

Paradigm

Paradigm is another way to classify a programming language. It is based upon the programming features supported by a language. Object-oriented (using objects), functional (using functions), structured (using loops and conditionals), and aspect-oriented (using modules) programming are a few examples of a paradigm. Many high-level languages — Python included — support multiple paradigms.

Integrated Development Environment (IDE)

It is a computer application that allows programmers to write, run, and debug their software codes. Some of them are language-specific; others work with almost any language out there. Notepad++ and Sublime Text are notable examples of IDEs.

Package

Open-source packages are often rebundled by third-party contributors and released for public use. They are targeted for specific applications and usually have specialized modules added for that purpose.

32-bit and 64-bit Computer Systems

Although 64-bit computer systems were introduced in 1961, the first home computers to have this capability came to market in 2000 and didn't become common until recently. Better hardware architecture resulted in cost-effective design of 64-bit processing units. These systems offer faster processing and larger memory as compared to the older 32-bit processing units. It paved the way for a new era of software products that were not acutely hampered by memory and hardware limitations.

Character Encoding

Text is created with characters, and every language has a different set of characters. Computers rely on several special character-encoding sets to support as many characters as possible.

In the programming world, it's important to remember that each character is stored uniquely in memory. Even if two of them look the same to humans, they might relay completely different meanings to a computer due to the encoding used for them.

Dependency

Every object relies on something to function properly. For instance, your car depends on gas to run. You rely on oxygen to live or an alarm clock to wake up in the morning. Some dependencies are optional, such as the alarm clock, but others are compulsory, such as the oxygen in the air.

Brief History of Programming Languages

The journey of programming languages is centuries old. There are evidences of machine language programs as old as 1843 when Ada Lovelace wrote a mechanical computer algorithm. Here's a brief history of programming languages.

FORmula TRANslation (FORTRAN)

FORTRAN is an IBM endeavor that was launched in the 1950s. Program codes were written on punch cards and manually fed into the computers. The effort and finance it required to code and maintain the computers and programs at the time meant that the systems were limited to government agencies and global enterprises.

Pascal

Developed by Niklaus Wirth during the 1970s, it was based on Algorithmic Language 1960 (ALGOL 60). The purpose of this language was to teach the best coding practices to new programmers. It became famous and widely used commercially until it was slowly replaced by C language during the 1980s.

C

Dennis Ritchie created C language in 1972 and was one of the very first general-purpose languages that remains mainstream. It resulted in the family of programming languages that includes C++ and Objective C. Despite being a compiler language, it can help people hone their programming skills.

Perl

In 1987, Larry Wall of Unisys developed this language based on C for the sole purpose of working with text files. It was supposed to be named Pearl, but that was already taken, so Larry had to settle with Perl. Now, everyone would refer to it as a combination of two languages. It still has many general-purpose utilizations as well, such as web development, network programming, and system administration.

Ruby

The only language in the list whose creator is an Asian, Ruby was designed by Yukirhiro Matsumoto in 1993. Influenced by Perl and Basic, Yukihiro created a language that made programming enjoyable to bring masses into productive coding. Fun fact: Ruby is very similar to Python when it comes to syntax.

Java

Java was created by James Gosling of Sun Microsystems in 1995 and became part of the company's Java platform. Despite being under proprietary licenses, it is the most extensively used language today. The biggest reason behind this widespread popularity was Java platform's system independence. Sun Microsystems was taken over by Oracle in 2010, and Java has become their property since then.

Personal Home Page (PHP)

PHP is an open-source programming language created by Rasmus Lerdorf in 1995 to build websites. Global enterprises usually stay away from open-source tools, but PHP is truly an exception. Most website developers start their career through it. It is used to run the background processes of a website and help the website communicate with other parts of the internet.

JavaScript

Developed by Brendah Eich in 1995, JavaScript was heavily influenced by Java. It is the core component of the World Wide Web along with HTML and CSS. It gives websites the dynamic edge and is supported by every browser. Recently, word processors and PDF documents have started embedding JavaScript to support rich content as well.

Python

Python is a general-purpose, high-level language released in 1991 by Guido van Rossum. It is an interpreted language, though it also supports compiled system.

Even with so many languages available in the market, programming was still cumbersome as languages were machine-oriented. There was a need for a new version that's easier to read so that novice programmers could learn and code quickly. Thanks to Guido, that problem was solved.

The main purpose of Python is to enhance readability, which is evident by the use of whitespace to separate program lines. There are many Python environments available now. Due to it being open source, the Python community grew very quickly. This led to the development of an extensive list of external modules, some of which were later added to the core language as libraries.

These resources also gave Python the ability to integrate with other languages seamlessly. You would be in Python environment but writing code in Visual Basic, and Python will execute it straight away. You'll work on this in later chapters, but in the future, when you do the same in any other language, you'll understand why Python is so powerful.

Object-Oriented Programming (OOP)

Up until now, I have been avoiding talking about arguably the biggest programming concept conceived in the 20th century. Any guesses? Yes, you are right! It is object-oriented programming. Still, let's discuss it now before starting to work with Python.

What Is an Object and How Does OOP Work?

Consider a real-life scenario: you have a dog named Leo who loves it when you ask him to hug you. You also know the helpless face that

Leo makes when you ask him to mow the lawn because you are too tired. He genuinely wants to help, but it's beyond his capabilities.

In object-oriented programming, your dog is an object. You give a command to Leo when you ask him to hug you, and Leo complies because he recognizes the command. On the other hand, if you order a task that he doesn't understand, such as mowing the lawn, it leads to an error.

Objects were created to simplify coding numerous entities and controlling their behavior in humongous environments. For example, if you are developing a game, all characters are unique instances of the same object, so they have common characteristics. This makes it easier to group their actions and responses. The alternative would have been to code every character, as well as their actions and responses separately. Of course, this is unsustainable when creating big environments.

Python does support object-oriented programming. However, depending on what goal you are trying to accomplish, you may not do it extensively. As you'll find out later in this book, there are other programming techniques that suit different requirements better.

How to recognize if you are invoking object-oriented side of Python, you may ask? You need to use a command that looks like this:

```
object.command()
```

In our previous example, here's how the command will appear:

```
leo.hugme()
```

The hugme() command is referred to as a method. It might be unique to the object leo.

There are many integral programming concepts that every programmer should know about, irrespective of which languages they are learning. To avoid repetition, we are going to scrutinize them when we learn more about Python later.

Exercises

1. Go to convertbinary.com and get the binary code for "This is

the best book ever!"

2. Find a text to hexadecimal converter online and get the hexadecimal code for "This is the best book ever!"
3. When was Python created?
4. Who created the Pascal programming language?
5. Is Python a low-level language?
6. Have you seen a punch card ever?
7. Which language was made for processing text files?
8. Who invented Basic programming language? (Hint: You might want to get help from Google for this.)
9. You are going to the Bahamas for vacation. Write an algorithm for the entire process.
10. Create a flowchart for the algorithm that you wrote for Question 6.

CHAPTER TWO

STARTING WITH PYTHON

P ython creator Guido van Rossum is also dubbed as the Benevolent Dictator for Life (BDFL) because he single-handedly spearheaded Python's development from the start until 2018. Now, he's a part of a Steering Council that comprises of five members. This helped to keep Python developing in a systematic way even when many customized versions of it were launched by different platforms over the years.

Before Python, only C language had properly formatted block comments, but it didn't support inline comments. The other famous language at the time, Perl, was famous for being ugly. Python started the enhanced readability revolution that many languages adopted later on. It focused on making programming language easier to read and comprehend for humans. It opened doors to casual programmers who greatly benefited the programming field in the long-term.

Python also helped with code reusability and recycling. Instead of programming everything from scratch, programmers can easily understand others' work and use them as reference. The open-source nature of Python project was immensely useful here, too. Another feature that greatly enhanced readability was the proper support for both inline comments and comment blocks.

The official Python website is https://www.python.org/. It contains all the releases for various operating systems. A comprehensive documentation is also available on the website. The community section has links to Python forums that will be helpful when you pursue advanced skills.

Python 2.x vs. 3.x

On October 2000, Python 2.0 was released with many new features that changed the language to a great extent. The changes proved to be worthwhile, and the popularity of the language grew immensely in the programming community. Python 2.7 is arguably the best and definitely the most widely used version of Python to date. It supported integration with almost any platform but kept the syntax easy to learn.

Python 3.0 was released in 2008, meanwhile, and it was another major update. They made sweeping changes to even basic syntax. It wasn't entirely backward-compatible, which drew mixed opinions in the Python community. Even though the new version came with a porting utility that provided limited extent support in converting 2.x codes to 3.x, many people stuck with Python 2.7 and still remain loyal to it. Initially, support for 2.7 version was set to end in 2015 but was extended to 2020. Even now, it's evident that 2.7 is not going anywhere.

For the purpose of teaching programming basics and starting with Python in this book, we have chosen the 2.7 platform. It is easier to understand and simpler to code; there is so much resource material available to develop skills quickly, too. You can learn Python 3 at your own pace when you feel comfortable doing so. You'll also see that the changes aren't too troublesome if you already have a good grasp on the language.

Choosing a Python Environment

In this book, we are going to use Windows 10 operating system as our platform as most people are familiar with it. The traditional release for Windows is available for download from the official Python website, nicknamed CPython. Several third-party Python implementations are also available for 32-bit and 64-bit Windows systems, each offering additional benefits.

Furthermore, we are going to work with Python 2.7, which was developed by ActiveState, and complement it with Mark Hammond's re-packaged PythonWin. I would like to say special thanks to Mark Hammond here for his years of dedication and hard work without which Python on Windows might never would have lasted long.

Why this combination, you may ask? In truth, the official Python package has a very lackluster IDE. ActiveState offers extra libraries while PythonWin has a colorful IDE. The combination, therefore, makes coding fun for beginners.

It is useful to know at this point that there are different free IDEs available for Python like Notepad++ and Sublime Text 3 that look quite nice. However, it's a little complex to run codes written with them. Once you are comfortable with Python, you can choose the implementation and IDE that you feel at home with.

Installing and Setting Up Python

This section can prove to be a bit overwhelming, maybe more than the actual coding, for the simple fact that it is all new to you. Don't worry, there's no need to hurry. Read through the steps below at your own pace.

Step 1

The first step is to find out if you have a 32-bit or 64-bit computer so that you can install the correct version of Python. If you already know what you have, please skip to the next step.

Click on the Windows icon on the bottom left corner of your screen. Type "system" in the white search bar at the bottom and click on "System Information" app that shows up.

In the new window, look for "System Type" and check the value in the column next to it. It will tell you if you have a 32-bit or 64-bit system.

Step 2

To get the Windows installer for ActiveState Python, officially and more famously known as ActivePython, go to this link: https://www.activestate.com/products/activepython/downloads/ Select the ActivePython 2.7 to get redirected to the signup page. After creating a free account, download the 32-bit or 64-bit Windows installer that's compatible with your computer system. It is usually installed in a Python27 folder in the root directory C:\Python27\. You can change the installation path but make sure to note the folder where you install Python.

An important point to remember here is to never use spaces when creating a folder or subfolder that will contain programming files. Also, you must check the option "Add Python to Register" — it'll make future module and package installations much easier.

After ActivePython is installed, go to this link to download PythonWin: https://github.com/mhammond/pywin32/releases Download the latest 32-bit or 64-bit installer for your computer and start the installation. Make sure that the folder is the same where you installed ActivePython. If you checked the option "Add Python to Register" during ActivePython installation, the folder will be pre-filled but always guarantee that it's the same path where you installed ActivePython.

Once the installation is done, go to the folder where you installed ActivePython. If you didn't change the path during the process, it'll be C:\Python27\Lib\site-packages\PythonWin and find the file

PythonWin.exe. Click the right button on the mouse to launch it and select "Send to > Desktop (create shortcut)." Now, you can always start Python straight from your desktop.

Writing and Running Your First Program

What Is a Module?

In Python, a module is any file with an extension '.py' that contains program lines. You can write your own modules and save them to run later or call in another one. You can download and install a third-party module to extend the capabilities of Python to code for a specific task.

Once the installation and setup of Python environment is complete, press the right button on your mouse twice to open the PythonWin icon on your desktop. A new window will appear, similar to this one:

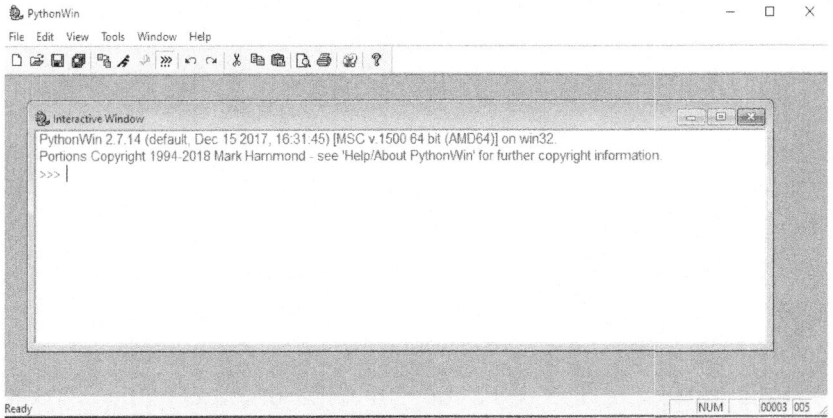

If you accidentally close the "Interactive Window," you can reopen it by clicking this icon:

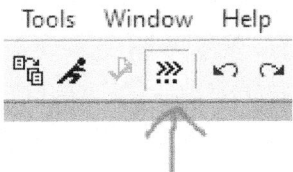

It's time to learn about a decades-old tradition in the programming community. The first thing that any programmer should learn to write should always be "Hello, world" in a programming language. This tradition was set by Dennis Ritchie and Brian Kernighan when they did the same while testing the development of the C language.

It is 2019, though, and programming has outgrown our world. There are satellites in outer space that are purely controlled through automated programs. It is time to accept that computers and programs have reached places where no human has ever gone and may never will. For that reason, it is time to know how to write "Hello, Universe!" instead. Type the following line after the >>> prompt and hit Enter:

    print "Hello, Universe!"

Python will run the command and show the following:

Congratulations, you instructed Python to follow your command without any mistake! However, there's one more thing to learn here. We are going to save our very first module so that we can run it later or anytime we want.

Click on the 'New' icon. You'll see a pop-up with three options: Python Script, Grep, and Pychecker. Python Script will be selected by default; just press the 'OK' button without deselecting it. A new blank window will open.

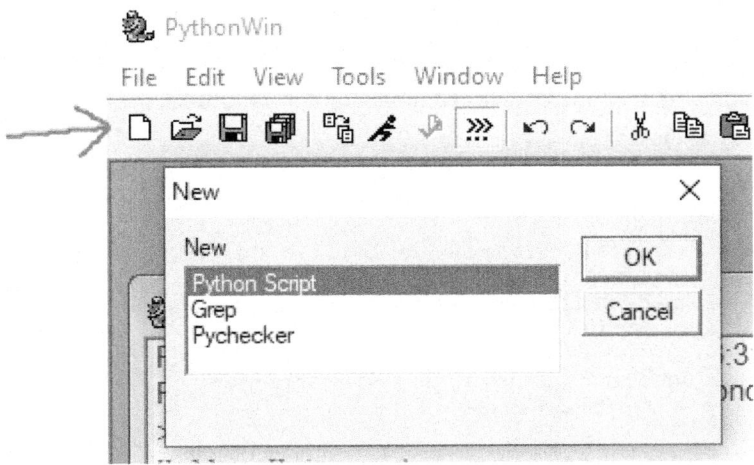

Copy the following line of code in the blank window and click on the 'Save' icon:

```
print "Hello, Universe!"
```

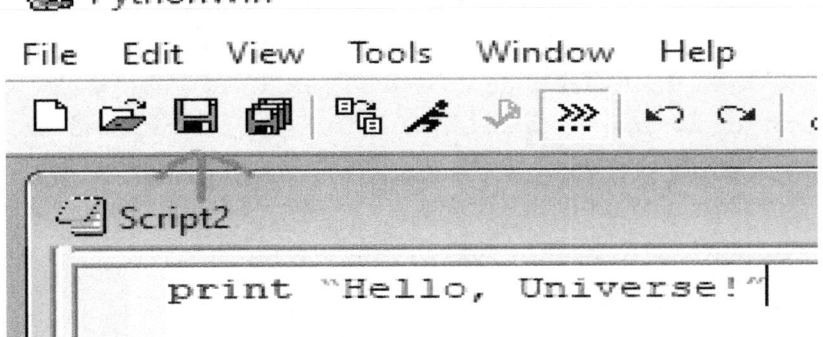

You will see an option to choose folder and filename when you try to save this module. Select the folder where you installed Python preferably and name the file as 'hello-universe.py' accordingly. You can create a subfolder to keep your own program codes organized and separate from Python's default files. Note that just like folder names, we did not use space in the filename. Never ever add spaces in a program filename or folder in any language even if the documentation says that the programming language supports spaces it. It will save you from a lot of trouble and headaches in the long run.

Bonus: Beware of copying and pasting the code from sources other than a Python file with the '.py' extension. It might read the same, but the characters might have different encoding. This will lead to the following error when you try to save such a module:

File save failed

Encoding failed:
'latin-1' codec can't encode character u'\u201c' in position 6: ordinal not in range(256)
Please add desired source encoding as first line of file, eg
-*- coding: mbcs -*-

If you continue, the file will be saved as binary and will not be valid in the declared encoding.

Save the file as binary with an invalid encoding?

| Yes | No |

Once the program is saved, close the window that now says 'hello-universe.py'. Then, click the 'Run' icon. You can hit 'Browse' to navigate to the folder where you have saved 'hello-universe.py' file. Select the file and click the 'Open' button. The file path will now be filled in the field besides "Script File". You can ignore all other options for now and click 'OK'. As soon as you do so, Python will read and execute the 'hello-universe.py' module.

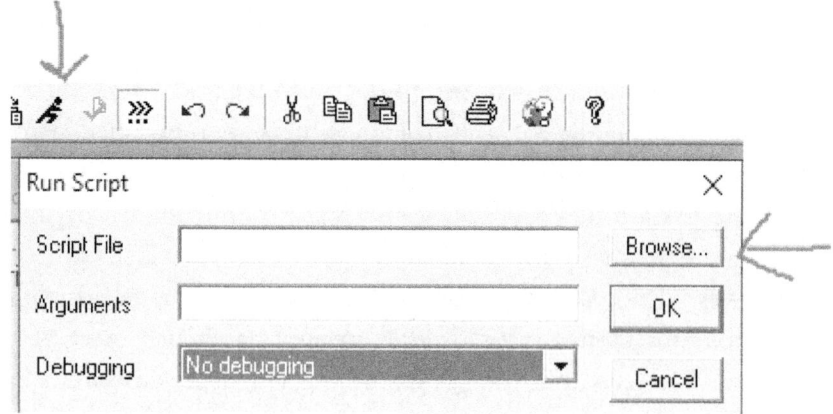

The Python interpreter "Interactive Window" will show the following output:

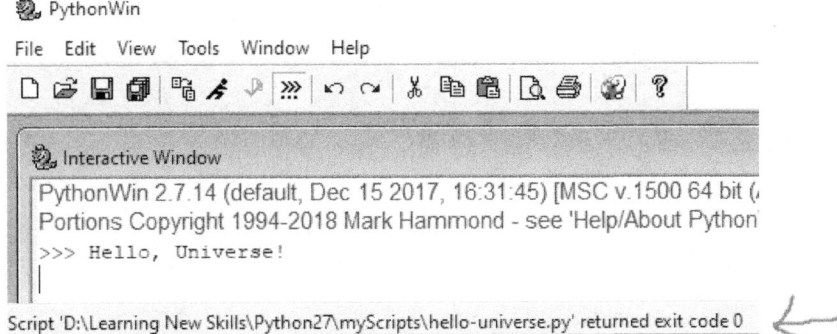

Pay special attention to the log entry at the bottom that says, "...returned exit code 0". It means that the program ran successfully without any errors. Bravo! You have now saved and ran your first programming module in Python without a glitch.

Installing Optional External Modules

What Is a Package? What Is Import?

Sometimes when third-party contributors write codes to add special functionality to Python, they have to break them into several modules. Those are structured together to create a package that makes it easier to distribute. The process of calling a module that you created — or an external package you installed — in your program is called import. Thanks to the open-source nature of Python project, there hasn't been any shortage of contributors over the years. This gives Python the ability to become extended through modules and packages to create solutions for complex tasks.

Pip — Your Best Friend

You can install external packages with the help of Python's package manager (and your best friend), pip. To illustrate how to use it, we are going to install a package named Scrapy, one of the most popular packages in Python to scrape websites. We could have done this by running the commands in the PythonWin interpreter "Interactive Window", but we are going to use Windows command prompt to show how easy it is to run Python commands on an operating system interface.

1. Click the Windows icon at the bottom left side of you screen.
2. Click the search bar at the bottom and type "Command Prompt".
3. Hit the right-click button on the first option and select "Run as administrator". A new window will pop up with a black background.
4. Type the following command and hit Enter:

```
python -m pip install scrapy
```

As soon as you do that, Python will start downloading and installing the package. You'll be able to see a progress bar, as well as several messages updating you on the process. In the end, you'll see a message that says, "Successfully installed…" You can now close the window by clicking the X icon on the top-right corner of the command prompt window or typing the following command:

```
exit
```

Here's how the entire process looks like if completed successfully.

```
Administrator: Command Prompt

Microsoft Windows [Version 10.0.18362.295]
(c) 2019 Microsoft Corporation. All rights reserved.

C:\WINDOWS\system32>python -m pip install scrapy
Collecting scrapy
  Downloading https://files.pythonhosted.org/packages/29/4b/585e8e111ffb01466c59281f34febb13
    100% |################################| 235kB 2.4MB/s
Collecting parsel>=1.5 (from scrapy)
  Downloading https://files.pythonhosted.org/packages/86/c8/fc5a2f9376066905dfcca334da2a2584
Requirement already satisfied: service-identity in d:\learning new skills\python27\lib\site-
Requirement already satisfied: Twisted>=13.1.0; python_version != "3.4" in d:\learning new s
Requirement already satisfied: lxml; python_version != "3.4" in d:\learning new skills\pytho
Requirement already satisfied: six>=1.5.2 in d:\learning new skills\python27\lib\site-package
Collecting w3lib>=1.17.0 (from scrapy)
  Downloading https://files.pythonhosted.org/packages/6a/45/1ba17c50a0bb16bd950c9c2b92ec60d4
Requirement already satisfied: pyOpenSSL in d:\learning new skills\python27\lib\site-package
Collecting PyDispatcher>=2.0.5 (from scrapy)
  Downloading https://files.pythonhosted.org/packages/cd/37/39aca520918ce1935bea9c356bcbb7ed
Collecting queuelib (from scrapy)
  Downloading https://files.pythonhosted.org/packages/4c/85/ae64e9145f39dd6d14f8af3fa809a270
Collecting cssselect>=0.9 (from scrapy)
  Downloading https://files.pythonhosted.org/packages/3b/d4/3b5c17f00cce85b9a1e6f91096e1cc8e
Requirement already satisfied: functools32; python_version < "3.0" in d:\learning new skills
Requirement already satisfied: pyasn1 in d:\learning new skills\python27\lib\site-packages (
Requirement already satisfied: attrs in d:\learning new skills\python27\lib\site-packages (f
Requirement already satisfied: pyasn1-modules in d:\learning new skills\python27\lib\site-pa
Requirement already satisfied: Automat>=0.3.0 in d:\learning new skills\python27\lib\site-pa
Requirement already satisfied: constantly>=15.1 in d:\learning new skills\python27\lib\site-
Requirement already satisfied: zope.interface>=3.6.0 in d:\learning new skills\python27\lib\
Requirement already satisfied: hyperlink>=17.1.1 in d:\learning new skills\python27\lib\site
Requirement already satisfied: incremental>=16.10.1 in d:\learning new skills\python27\lib\s
Requirement already satisfied: cryptography>=2.1.4 in d:\learning new skills\python27\lib\si
Requirement already satisfied: setuptools in d:\learning new skills\python27\lib\site-packag
Requirement already satisfied: idna>=2.1 in d:\learning new skills\python27\lib\site-package
Requirement already satisfied: cffi>=1.7; platform_python_implementation != "PyPy" in d:\lea
Requirement already satisfied: enum34; python_version < "3" in d:\learning new skills\python
Requirement already satisfied: asn1crypto>=0.21.0 in d:\learning new skills\python27\lib\sit
Requirement already satisfied: ipaddress; python_version < "3" in d:\learning new skills\pyt
Requirement already satisfied: pycparser in d:\learning new skills\python27\lib\site-package
Building wheels for collected packages: PyDispatcher
  Running setup.py bdist_wheel for PyDispatcher ... done
  Stored in directory: C:\Users\danis\AppData\Local\pip\Cache\wheels\88\99\96\cfef6665f9cb15
Successfully built PyDispatcher
Installing collected packages: cssselect, w3lib, parsel, PyDispatcher, queuelib, scrapy
Successfully installed PyDispatcher-2.0.5 cssselect-1.1.0 parsel-1.5.2 queuelib-1.5.0 scrapy
You are using pip version 9.0.1, however version 19.2.3 is available.
You should consider upgrading via the 'python -m pip install --upgrade pip' command.

C:\WINDOWS\system32>
```

Bonus: You can convert Windows command prompt to Python interpreter environment. Simply open the Windows command prompt and type the following command to let Python take over:

```
python
```

The window will look like this after the execution:

Command Prompt - python

```
c:\Windows\System32>python
ActivePython 2.7.14.2717 (ActiveState Software Inc.) based on
Python 2.7.14 (default, Dec 15 2017, 16:31:45) [MSC v.1500 64 bit (AMD64)] on win32
Type "help", "copyright", "credits" or "license" for more information.
>>>
```

Note that it shows the ActivePython interface and not the PythonWin IDE interface. To exit from Python and resume Windows command prompt interface, type:

exit()

Exercises

1. Are we using Windows- or Linux-based platform to learn Python?
2. Which Python environment did we setup in this chapter?
3. Who has contributed to the Python project for decades to keep it running on Windows?
4. List down at least three popular Python implementations or re-packages.
5. List down at least three popular IDEs that you can use to write and debug Python code. The IDEs must be Python specific.
6. What is the name of the Python's package manager?
7. Print "Hello, Universe!" after converting Windows command prompt to Python and then exit.
8. Print your full name on Python's "Interactive Window".
9. Write a module to do the task of Q1.
10. Try installing the famous external module pywin32 using Windows command prompt.

CHAPTER THREE

PYTHON BASICS

I n Chapter 2, we ran a simple command to make sure everything is perfectly setup. If you remember, back in chapter 1, we were discussing programming concepts. It's time to learn about them along with Python basics.

Building Blocks

Variables

Consider an empty box in your basement that you can use to store anything. The basement is like your computer's memory and that empty box is a variable. You can have as many boxes as you can fit in there, but do not forget that you need some space for other stuff as well.

It's the same with variables. It is known as such because you can change its value whenever you want. You can assign data to variables; the instruction is called assignment statement. In older programming languages, you had to first reserve space in memory by declaring the variable name and it's type before you could use it in your program. In modern languages like Python, you don't worry about all those things. Having said that, it is a good idea to know about the underlying concepts.

On the Python interpreter, try the following code. Press Enter after each line.

```
a = 4
print a
```

The first line a = 4 is an assignment statement. The symbol '=' is the assignment operator. We assigned the integer value of 4 to the variable a. Then, in the second statement, we instructed Python to print the value of variable a.

You can use any name for a variable, but you need to keep certain rules in mind.

1. The first letter of a variable name must be an alphabet.
2. You can use numbers for subsequent letters in a variable name.
3. You can use uppercase and lower alphabets in a variable name.
4. The first letter alphabet can be an uppercase letter, but it's inadvisable. We'll discuss the reason later.
5. Underscore (_) is the only symbol that can be used in a variable name.

Do you remember the keywords in chapter 1? Those are special words that a programming language reserves for operational purposes that you can't use as a variable name. Python has 31 keywords in total, namely:

1. and
2. as
3. assert
4. break
5. class
6. continue
7. def
8. del

9. elif
10. else
11. except
12. exec
13. finally
14. for
15. from
16. global
17. if
18. import
19. in
20. is
21. lambda
22. not
23. or
24. pass
25. print
26. raise
27. return
28. try
29. while
30. with
31. yield

Here's an example of declaring and assigning a string variable.

```
hell0 = "I am fine, thank you"
```

Here's an example of declaring a float variable.

```
fltpi = 3.14
```

This is a string assignment.

```
fltpistr = "3.14"
```

If you want to type a variable, you can use the type() method. Enter the following line of code and see the result in Python interpreter:

```
type(fltpistr)
```

The output will indicate that the variable fltpistr contains a string value.

```
<type 'str'>
```

Constants

As the name suggests, constants are data values that have a fixed meaning and can't be changed through programming. For example, number 21 is a constant. It means that the number 21 can't be number 20 or anything else.

Statements

Every instruction that the Python interpreter can execute is called a statement. A program is mostly a sequence of statements. So far, we have seen two statements: print and assignment. As you might have noticed, the assignment statement doesn't produce any output. On the other hand, print statement's sole purpose is to output data.

Let's have a little fun, shall we? Type the following statements in Python and press Enter after each line.

```
num = 123
num = num + 7
print num
```

Did you get confused by the num = num + 7 statement? How can num be equal to num + 7? Remember, '=' is not an equal sign but an assignment operator. In Python, the right side of the operator '=' is calculated first, and the resultant value is assigned to the variable name on the left. It is the reason why the following statement will produce a syntax error. Give it a try.

```
13 = numerr
```

Congratulations! By the way, you have produced the first syntax error in your Python's history. Let's try one more thing now.

```
print 1,22,333
```

I am pretty sure that you are looking at the output and wondering, "What's that?" Here it is:

```
>>> print 1,22,333
1 22 333
```

Awesome work! You have produced the first semantic error. You used commas in a way that even though it is the correct way in real-life, it produced wrong results because Python treats commas between numbers in a completely different way.

Here's the lesson: If you put commas in between numbers, Python will think that it is a list of different comma-separated numbers. If you want Python to treat it as a single number, you should remove the commas. So, the following statement will produce the right result:

```
print 122333
```

End of Statements

Many programming languages use semicolon (;) to create boundary between two lines of code. This helps in writing multiple statements in one horizontal line. Like Basic, Python uses a new line (Enter) to separate statements in line with its philosophy of enhanced readability. This also means that Python wants the programmer to keep the statements shorter even if you have to write a few extra statements to get the job done.

However, there will be times when your statement will not fit in one display line no matter how hard you try. In such situations, you can use the backslash (\) to tell Python that the next line is a continuation of the previous one. For example, below lines of code is a single valid Python statement. Press Enter after each line.

```
>>> brkr = \
... 36 + \
... 143
```

Notice the three dots that the Python interpreter adds to show that it's waiting for the next part of the statement. You can test if the statement ran correctly by checking the value of variable brkr. The returned value should be 179.

```
>>> brkr
179
```

Expressions

Expressions are combinations of constants, variables, and operators that will return a result in interpreter mode but will not work when writing a module. For example, in "Interactive Window", input number 5 and press Enter and Python will print it.

>>> 5
5

When writing a module, if you only write 5, Python will not output 5 when executing the module. There are a few expressions that can work standalone, but that's to be discussed in a later topic. For now, remember that expressions usually appear on the right side of an assignment statement.

Operators

Operators are special characters that represent mathematical computations. The data points which the operator is applied to are known as operands. The operands can be constants, variables or expressions. Python supports a wide range of operators, such as:

Arithmetic Operators

1. Addition (+) - adds the operands
2. Subtraction (-) - subtracts one operand from the other
3. Multiplication (*) - multiplies all operands
4. Division (/) - divides one operand with the other
5. Modulus (%) - divides and returns the remainder
6. Exponential (**) - calculates exponential values

Comparative Operators

1. (==) - compare if two operands are equal
2. (!=) - compare if two operands are not equal - (<>) is similar
3. (>) - if one operand is greater than the other - (>=) is greater than or equal to
4. (<) - if one operand is smaller than the other - (<=) is less than or equal to

Logical Operators

1. and - Logical AND - true if both operands are true
2. or - Logical OR - true if any operand is true
3. not - Logical NOT - negate the operation it precedes

Assignment Operator

1. (=) - calculate value of right side operands and assign to left side operand

One important rule to remember here is the order of operation. If an expression has more than one operator.3, which operation will be given precedence? Python follows the PEMDAS rules of precedence that mathematics follows.

1. The highest precedence belongs to Parentheses. You can use them to change the order of operation the way you want. Parentheses are sometimes also used to enhance readability in a long expression.
2. Exponentiation has the second highest precedence.
3. Multiplication and Division have the same precedence.
4. Addition and subtraction have the same precedence.

In case multiple operators have the same precedence in an expression, they are evaluated with respect to the left-to-right rule. Let's work with a few examples.

```
>>> 350 + ( 250 * ( 3 - 1 ) ) + ( 350 * 2 )
1550
>>> 7 % 4
3
>>> mon = 2450
>>> mon * ( mon / mon )
2450
```

We are going to see some more on these operators in the exercises.

Conditionals

With conditional statements, operators are applied on operands to make a decision on the flow of program execution. The operands can be a variable, constant, or an expression. The flow of execution of a program can be controlled with these statements, commonly known as control flow.

The if statement

With the if statement, the programmer tells Python to test a condition. In case the result is true, execute the statements inside the if statement. Here's how you can test a simple if statement.

```
>>> n = 179
>>> if n == 188:
```

After this, Python will start outputting the three dots when you hit Enter after entering a statement to indicate that the statements are inside the if statement block. To get out of the if statement, press Enter again. The whole process looks like this on the Python Interactive Window:

```
>>> n = 179
>>> if n == 188:
...     print "That's not right!"
...
>>>
```

No output? Don't worry; it is because the print statement didn't run. The variable n was assigned 179; that's why the condition if n == 188 turned out of the false. It meant that the print statement never got executed. The code block inside the if statement is automatically indented to the right, so it's easier to understand which statements will be executed in case the if statement condition is true. Python uses indentation to mark different blocks of code. If you have read Python documentation, these blocks are referred to as suites.

Now, what happens if the condition is true? Let's try our last piece of code with a small modification.

```
>>> n = 179
>>> if n == 179:
...     print "That's not right!"
...
"That's not right!"
>>>
```

This time, we see an output on our screen because the if condition if n == 179 was true.

The question is, can you run a code block when the if condition is false? Yes, you can. Here comes the else clause to the rescue.

```
>>> xcon = 33
>>> if xcon < 25:
...     print "xcon is smaller"
... else:
...     print "xcon is larger"
...
xcon is larger
>>>
```

The variable xcon is assigned the value of 33. The if condition is false, which leads to the statement under else clause to be executed. There's another clause elif, which is short for else if. Here's an example of that.

```
>>> xcon = 33
>>> if xcon < 25:
...     print "xcon is smaller"
... elif xcon > 30:
...     print "xcon is larger"
... else:
...     print "couldn't determine"
...
xcon is larger
>>>
```

You can also nest if statements like this:

```
>>> ynest = 147
>>> znext = "Test"
>>> if znext == "Test":
...     if ynest > 200:
...             print "ynest out of range"
...     elif ynest < 100:
...             print "ynest too low"
...     else:
...             print "ynest within range"
... else:
...     print "out of scope"
...
ynest within range
>>>
```

This results in an output of ynest within range.

Thanks to the logical operators, you can combine multiple expressions in if statement. Let's look at the example below.

```
>>> ynest = 147
>>> znext = "Test"
>>> if znext == "Result" and ynest == 147:
...     print "Both conditions are true"
... else:
...     print "It's a fail"
...
It's a fail
```

>>>

In the example above, the znext == "Result" was false. It made the entire expression in the if statement to return false. Remember, and operator will return false even if only one of the operands is false. It resulted in the statement under else to be executed hence the output of "It's a fail".

Bonus: Unlike other popular languages, Python doesn't have a switch-case statement. You can create your own version of switch-case, but it's not necessary, so we'll skip it to keep things from becoming complicated too soon. The lesson to remember here is that the if-else-elif conditional statements are your only source of control flow in the Python language.

Basic Data Types

Python supports various data types. Some of them are described below.

Numbers

Every programming language supports numbers, and Python is no exception.

Integer

A whole number can be either positive or negative. Here's an example.

```
xint = 100099
```

Floating point

A number comes with a decimal point. Below is an example.

```
yflt = 10.0099
```

Long integers

It is an exceptionally long number that can be represented using octal or hexadecimal notation. This is a little tricky, but take note the trailing "L" in the sample number below.

zlon = 1278495467868413514541L

Complex

Python can also handle imaginary numbers.

cjimg = (5+9j)

Strings

The alphanumeric combination of characters that can also include special characters is known as string. They are easily identifiable because they are enclosed within double quotes or sometimes within single quotes. We'll look into strings in detail very soon.

Taking Input

In Python 2.7, there are two ways of taking input from user. Let's take a look at both of them.

The input() Function

The input() is actually not used in production coding because it's not secure. This function processes whatever user has entered. If it's a statement, it executes the statement. It gives user access to perform actions that it shouldn't have. It is also impossible to get a string through the input() function. Let's look at the alternative.

The raw_input() Function

This function is used to take a string input from the user. Here's an example:

```
>>> username = raw_input("Enter your name: ")
```

Running this line of code will result in a popup with the prompt

"Enter your name: ". The entered value will be saved in the variable username. However, it raises the question, "Is there a way to get numbers as input from the user?" Yes, you can use raw_input and string to integer conversion.

```
>>> input10 = raw_input("Enter a number: ")
>>> input10
'4877'
>>> input10_int = int(input10)
>>> input10_int
4877
```

Loops a.k.a. Iterations

Why were computers invented? The basic reason is to help humans do things that they are bad at, especially performing repetitive tasks. Therefore, loops are the primary ingredient of all programming languages. It enables programmers to execute the same code block as many times as necessary. Generally speaking, if you know the number of times a block should be executed, you should use a for loop. Otherwise, you can use a while loop.

The for loop

For loop is also called definite loop because you can only use it if you know the number of times the loop should execute beforehand. Before we look at an example, we have to understand two more concepts.

Iterable

Anything that can be used to iterate over in a for loop is called an iterable. It can be a range of numbers, a string, a list of values, or anything that has multiple values associated with it.

Iterator

An iterator is an entity that's assigned a value from iterable during a loop execution. It can either be used to keep count of the number of loops performed or contain the value that'll be used in the code block

within the for loop. Sometimes, both are performed.
Here's an example of a simple for loop.

```
>>> for i in range(1,10):
...     print i
...
1
2
3
4
5
6
7
8
9
>>>
```

A few pointers:

1. range() is a special function that can be used to iterate over numbers by defining the lower and upper limits.
2. The loop was broken as soon as the value of iterator became equal to the upper limit set in the range(). The code block inside the loop doesn't get run for that instance. So, if we want to print numbers 1 to 10, we will have to use range(1,11).

By default, range() uses an increment of 1. You can control that, but remember that you can only provide an integer value as an increment to the range(). Otherwise, you will get an error.

```
>>> for i in range(1,11,2):
...     print i
...
1
3
5
7
9
>>>
```

You can also not specify the lower for the range() if you like.

```
>>> for i in range(12):
...     print i
...
0
1
2
3
```

```
4
5
6
7
8
9
10
>>>
```

Notice how the numbering starts from 0. But in this scenario, you cannot give out a custom increment value. To use a custom increment, you'll have to give the lower limit even if it's a zero.

```
>>> for i in range(0,12,2):
...     print i
...
0
2
4
6
8
10
>>>
```

Bonus: What happens if you lower limit is greater than the upper limit. Do we get an error? Let's give it a try.

```
>>> for i in range(12,2):
...     print i
...
>>>
```

Surprising, isn't it? There's no error, just no output. That's because the loop initialized but got terminated before there was any possibility to execute the block inside the for loop. It gives the impression that the condition is checked at the start of each iteration. Otherwise, we would have seen at least on line of output on the screen.

The while loop

Also known as an indefinite loop for a very good reason that we'll check out soon, this loop is used when you don't know how many times a loop should run. Therefore, you use an expression to check for the specific condition when the loop iterations must stop. Here's a simple example of a while loop.

```
>>> count = 0
```

```
>>> while (count < 3):
...     print "Universe says hi!"
...     count = count + 1
...
Universe says hi!
Universe says hi!
Universe says hi!
>>>
```

A few important things to note:

1. You might be wondering why the output was printed three times when we used the condition count < 3. The reason is that we explicitly set count = 0 at the start. First iteration occured when count = 0, then once for count = 1, and then once more when count = 2. After that, the loop execution was broken.

2. You have to explicitly update the operand of the expression used in the while loop condition, as well as inside the loop. count = count + 1 is doing the exact operation. If you forget to do that, it'll result in an infinite loop because the value of variable count will always remain zero and the condition to break the loop count < 3 will never occur. In olden days, this would have led to a system crash. In modern computers, the system might not crash, but the program execution will definitely get stuck and your PythonWin window will become unresponsive. You'll have to force shutdown and restart PythonWin.

Bonus: After the loop execution, check the value of the count variable.

```
>>> count
3
```

Now, if you try to run the same while loop without resetting value of count to zero, Python will stop loop execution right away because the while condition count < 3 is false.

In short, be very careful when using a while loop. It's understood that certain situations will leave you without any alternative to using the while loop, but try to avoid it as much as you can until you are confident with your coding skills.

Just like conditional statements, loops can be nested. You can also use for and while loops together.

Lists

You cannot perform most string operations until you learn what a list means. Simply put, a list is a widely used data structure in Python. It is an equivalent of arrays in other programming languages. You can easily recognize a list because it's enclosed in brackets. Let's look at our first list below.

```
implist = ['7','coffee','omelette',9,'work']
```

As you can see, we can combine different data types inside a list. The position of each item in a list is called index. The first item has an index zero. It is important to remember that their positions are fixed. Here's how you can retrieve the first item of the list.

```
>>> implist[0]
'7'
```

You can get the number of items in a list using the len() function.

```
>>> len(implist)
5
```

We can use loops to iterate through a list. Here's an example of using a for loop on our list.

```
>>> for item in implist:
...     print item
...
7
coffee
omelette
9
work
```

Here, we used the associative operator "in" to get each item from the list. Let's go a few steps forward with the print statement to get output meaningful data.

```
>>> for item in implist:
...     print "Value:",item,"- Type:",type(item),"- Position:",implist.index(item)
...
Value: 7 - Type: <type 'str'> - Position: 0
Value: coffee - Type: <type 'str'> - Position: 1
Value: omelette - Type: <type 'str'> - Position: 2
Value: 9 - Type: <type 'int'> - Position: 3
Value: work - Type: <type 'str'> - Position: 4
```

To get the index of each item in the list, we have used the index()
method.

We can use a negative element to get the last item.

```
>>> implist[-1]
'work'
```

We can also change the value of any item in a list even if the types of
current and new data don't match.

```
>>> implist[3] = "Now it's 8am"
>>> implist
['7', 'coffee', 'omelette', "Now it's 8am", 'work']
```

We can use lists in conditions to check if a value is in a list to control
flow of execution.

```
>>> if "sleep" not in implist:
...     print "where's the fun in that"
...
where's the fun in that
```

We can also add new items in the list using the method append(). The
new item will be added at the end of the list.

```
>>> implist.append("lunch at 11")
>>> implist
['7', 'coffee', 'omelette', "Now it's 8am", 'work', 'lunch at 11']
```

If you want to add a new item at a specific index, use the inset()
method.

```
>>> implist.insert(1,"shower")
>>> implist
['7', 'shower', 'coffee', 'omelette', "Now it's 8am", 'work', 'lunch at 11']
```

The remove() method can be used to get rid of a specific item.

```
>>> implist.remove("omelette")
>>> implist
['7', 'shower', 'coffee', "Now it's 8am", 'work', 'lunch at 11']
```

To remove an item by it's index, we can use the pop() method.

```
>>> implist.pop(3)
"Now it's 8am"
>>> implist
['7', 'shower', 'coffee', 'work', 'lunch at 11']
```

If no index is provided in pop(), the last item is popped out of the
list.

There are various ways to join two lists. We are looking at one, the
extend() method.

```
>>> offlist = ["weekend","all fun", "no work", 247]
>>> implist.extend(offlist)
>>> implist
['7', 'shower', 'coffee', 'work', 'lunch at 11', 'weekend', 'all fun', 'no work', 247]
```

```
>>> offlist
['weekend', 'all fun', 'no work', 247]
```

The extend() method added all items from the list offlist to the end of implist. Note that the second list offlist remains the same.

Lastly, you can add a list inside a list.

```
>>> parentlist = [["this ","is ","awesome"],"3 items", 15, "characters"]
>>> parentlist[0]
['this ', 'is ', 'awesome']
```

Strings

We already know what strings are. One of the biggest edge of Python over other languages is its robust string manipulation. Python can process string operations very efficiently and quickly. You can run loops on, join, break, or convert a string, and these are just the highlights of dozens of other things you can do with strings. Let's learn some new tricks today.

```
>>> streg = "154"
>>> type(streg)
<type 'str'>
```

You can enclose any data type within double quotes, and Python will consider it as a string. Amazing, isn't it? Now, look at the following code.

```
>>> strex = "007"
>>> streg+strex
'154007'
```

When you try to "add" two strings, Python concatenates them, and the result is another string. But for this to happen, both variables should be string. If you try to "add" a string with a number, Python will throw a type error, indicating that the types of two operands don't match.

```
>>> intex = 007
>>> streg+intex
```

Traceback (most recent call last):

    File "<interactive input>", line 1, in <module>

    TypeError: cannot concatenate 'str' and 'int' objects

There's one possibility, though. If I convert variable intex to a string, it can then be concatenated with the string streg. How to convert an integer to a string, you may ask? Try this:

```
>>> str(intex)
'7'
```

It seems very simple, but there's a catch. Notice how the leading zeros have been removed from the output. This is a drawback when converting an integer to a string. Don't feel down because there's several workarounds to that. One of them is to use the zfill() method.

```
>>> str(intex).zfill(3)
'007'
```

To summarize, we can concatenate a string with an integer (as shown below).

```
>>> streg+str(intex).zfill(3)
'154007'
```

If you want to know how many characters are there in a string, you can use the len() function.

```
>>> longstr = "This string contains 34 characters"
>>> len(longstr)
34
```

Strings support sequence protocol. Meaning, you can sequence through the elements of a string. This is why we can combine len() with range() in a for loop to iterate over any string and access each character. Here's the sample code:

```
>>> for i in range(len(longstr)):
...     print longstr[i],
...
```

This string contains 34 characters

A few pointers:

1. We are using longstr[i] that's like treating a string as a list of characters and accessing each element of the list. We will learn about lists very soon, but for now, just keep note of the syntax.

2. We used a trailing comma (,) in the print statement. This instructs Python to use a single space between each output of the print statement. By default, Python adds a new line (Enter) after each print output. That would have made the output take at least one and a half page in this book.

There are at least half a dozen =ways to access each character in a string. For now, let's just take a look at one more method. Again, considering the string as a list of characters, we can use the associative operator "in" to iterate through a string. Here's an example:

```
>>> for char in longstr:
...     print char,
...
```

This string contains 34 characters

It is definitely a more concise way to get the same output. One thing to remember here is that the first character of the string is location zero. For example, here's the code to get the first character of the variable longstr.

```
>>> longstr[0]
'T'
```

Considering that, the last character will have a location that's one number less than the len() of the string. Here's an example:

```
>>> longstr[len(longstr)-1]
's'
```

Keeping all the above things in mind, we can also use a while loop to iterate through the characters of a string. Here's the code for the same string longstr:

```
>>> i = 0
>>> while i <= len(longstr) - 1:
...     print longstr[i],
...     i = i + 1
...
```

This string contains 34 characters

Note that we didn't need to place len(longstr) - 1 within parentheses because it is on the right side of an expression. It'll always be calculated first before getting compared with the value of variable i. For your own clarity, you can use parentheses, so the while statement will look like this, while i <= (len(longstr) - 1):. There will be no difference in the output.

Also, note the difference between the upper limit on for and while loops. In the for loop, we used len(longstr) as is. However, in the while loop, we used len(longstr) - 1.

String Slicing Operations

We can slice a string to create another string if we know the starting and ending locations. The format is pretty straightforward.
string[starting location:optional stopping location:optional step]
Let's apply the operation on our longstr variable.

```
>>> longstr[5::]
'string contains 34 characters'
```

The new string is sliced from the longstr starting from the location 5. Since we didn't provide a stopping location, it slices until it gets to the end of the string. Just like the range() function, we can supply an integer value as a step. By default, the step value is set to one.

If you provide a negative step value, it tells Python to sequence through the string in the reverse direction.

```
>>> longstr[::-1]
'sretcarahc 43 sniatnoc gnirts sihT'
This can be further used in a for loop to access each character of a string in reverse
direction. Here's how to do it:
>>> for char in longstr[::-1]:
...     print char,
...
s r e t c a r a h c   4 3   s n i a t n o c   g n i r t s   s i h T
```

This particular output doesn't make much sense, but this trick will come pretty handy when you are dealing with strings during advanced programming.

Splitting and Replacing Characters in a String

Python is an intelligent programming language. Here's one example.

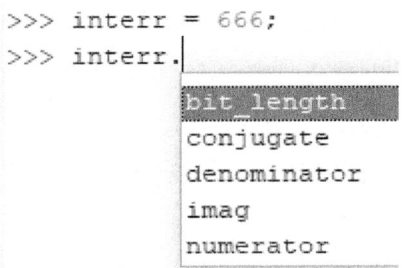

```
>>> interr = 666;
>>> interr.
        bit length
        conjugate
        denominator
        imag
        numerator
```

```
>>> longstr = "This string contains 34 characters"
>>> longstr.
```

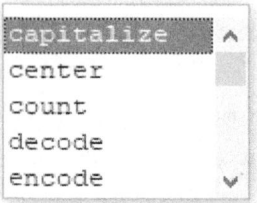

Do you notice the difference? Python interpreter recognizes the type of variable and considers it as an object because we put a dot (.) in the end. Thus, it shows only the appropriate methods.

Refresher: Do you remember object-oriented programming where everything is considered an object? By using split() and replace() methods, we are invoking the object-oriented side of Python. We didn't have to do anything special since combining different programming paradigms seamlessly is another power of Python.

Let's focus on the string method split().

```
>>> longstr.split()
```
['This', 'string', 'contains', '34', 'characters']

The split() method, as the name suggests, splits a string in positions where it finds a whitespace. We can pass a character to split() method, and it'll split the string wherever it finds the character in it. Here's an example.

```
>>> longstr.split("a")
```
['This string cont', 'ins 34 ch', 'r', 'cters']

Cool, right? Nowm, let's replace some characters in the longstr variable using the method replace().

```
>>> longstr.replace(" ","+")
```
'This+string+contains+34+characters'

We replaced all the spaces with a plus sign. Let's revert the changes.

```
>>> longstr.replace("+"," ")
```
'This string contains 34 characters'

Bonus: By default, replace() replaces all the occurrences of the existing characters with the desired one. Still, we can control it by telling Python how many occurrences it should replace.

```
>>> longstr.replace(" ","+", 2)
```
'This+string+contains 34 characters'

Only the first two occurrences of space are replaced with a plus sign. As you can see, the occurrences are counted from left to right.

Let's have one round of fun before we move to a different topic. We can use replace() to change any number of congruent characters with the desired characters.

```
>>> longstr.replace("contains","has")
'This string has 34 characters'
```

Have you ever used the find and replace tool on a word processor? See how easy it is to implement using Python.

More Data Structures

Dictionaries

Another powerful resource in Python, dictionaries are the objects of data structures. Unlike lists, where every item is referenced through it's index, every element has a key in a dictionary. This means that the elements inside a dictionary have no fixed positions. Searching individual elements in a dictionary is fast as Python doesn't have to iterate through the entire list to get to the desired item. With the help of the key, Python knows exactly where to look to get the right element from the dictionary.

On the other hand, there are some similarities between dictionaries and lists.

1. You can change the contents of a dictionary because it's mutable.
2. You can nest a dictionary inside another dictionary. In fact, one dictionary can contain an unlimited number of dictionaries.

You can easily identify a dictionary because it's enclosed in curly brackets, which is also called braces. Let's create a dictionary of Major League Soccer (MLS) team names as the values and their origin cities as the respective keys.

```
>>> mlsteams = {
```

```
... "Atlanta GA": "Atlanta United FC",
... "Bridgeview IL": "Chicago Fire",
... "Cincinnati OH": "FC Cincinnati",
... "Columbus OH": "Columbus Crew SC",
... "Washington DC": "DC United",
... "Montreal QC": "Montreal Impact",
... "Foxborough MA": "New England Revolution",
... "New York City NY": "New York City FC",
... "Harrison NJ": "New York Red Bulls",
... "Orlando FL": "Orlando City SC",
... "Chester PA": "Philadelphia Union",
... "Toronto ON": "Toronto FC"
... }
```

We can retrieve any element with its key.

```
>>> mlsteams["Toronto ON"]
'Toronto FC'
```

To check the length of a dictionary, we can use len(). It'll return the number of key-value pairs in the dictionary.

```
>>> len(mlsteams)
12
```

To get a list of all the keys, we can use the keys() method.

```
>>> mlsteams.keys()
['Harrison NJ', 'Orlando FL', 'Atlanta GA', 'Cincinnati OH', 'Washington DC',
'Foxborough MA', 'Montreal QC', 'Bridgeview IL', 'Toronto ON', 'New York City
NY', 'Columbus OH', 'Chester PA']
```

Similarly, to get a list of all the values, we can use the values() method.

```
>>> mlsteams.values()
['New York Red Bulls', 'Orlando City SC', 'Atlanta United FC', 'FC Cincinnati', 'DC
United', 'New England Revolution', 'Montreal Impact', 'Chicago Fire', 'Toronto FC',
'New York City FC', 'Columbus Crew SC', 'Philadelphia Union']
```

We can add a new key-value pair to the dictionary like this. We will use this opportunity to add a list as the new value.

```
>>> mlsteams["Future teams"] = ["Inter Miami CF","Nashville SC","Austin FC","St.
Louis"]
>>> mlsteams
{'Harrison NJ': 'New York Red Bulls', 'Orlando FL': 'Orlando City SC', 'Atlanta GA':
'Atlanta United FC', 'Cincinnati OH': 'FC Cincinnati', 'Washington DC': 'DC United',
'Foxborough MA': 'New England Revolution', 'Future teams': ['Inter Miami CF',
'Nashville SC', 'Austin FC', 'St. Louis'], 'Montreal QC': 'Montreal Impact',
'Bridgeview IL': 'Chicago Fire', 'Toronto ON': 'Toronto FC', 'New York City NY':
'New York City FC', 'Columbus OH': 'Columbus Crew SC', 'Chester PA':
'Philadelphia Union'}
```

Notice that the output key-value pairs are not in the order in which you entered them at the time of creating the dictionary.

You can use the key with method pop() to remove a key-value pair from the dictionary.

```
>>> mlsteams.pop("Future teams")
['Inter Miami CF', 'Nashville SC', 'Austin FC', 'St. Louis']
>>> mlsteams
{'Harrison NJ': 'New York Red Bulls', 'Orlando FL': 'Orlando City SC', 'Atlanta GA':
'Atlanta United FC', 'Cincinnati OH': 'FC Cincinnati', 'Washington DC': 'DC United',
'Foxborough MA': 'New England Revolution', 'Montreal QC': 'Montreal Impact',
'Bridgeview IL': 'Chicago Fire', 'Toronto ON': 'Toronto FC', 'New York City NY':
'New York City FC', 'Columbus OH': 'Columbus Crew SC', 'Chester PA':
'Philadelphia Union'}
```

There are various ways to loop through the key-value pairs in a dictionary. We'll test one such technique using the associative operator "in" to output both key and value.

```
>>> for city in mlsteams:
...     print "City:",city,"- Team:",mlsteams[city]
...
```

City: Harrison NJ - Team: New York Red Bulls

City: Orlando FL - Team: Orlando City SC

City: Atlanta GA - Team: Atlanta United FC

City: Cincinnati OH - Team: FC Cincinnati

City: Washington DC - Team: DC United

City: Foxborough MA - Team: New England Revolution

City: Montreal QC - Team: Montreal Impact

City: Bridgeview IL - Team: Chicago Fire

City: Toronto ON - Team: Toronto FC

City: New York City NY - Team: New York City FC

City: Columbus OH - Team: Columbus Crew SC

City: Chester PA - Team: Philadelphia Union

We can check if a key exists in the dictionary like this.

```
>>> if "Carson CA" in mlsteams:
...     print "defunct team present in the data"
... else:
...     print "data is clean"
...
```

data is clean

There are various ways to check if a value is present in the dictionary. Here's one of them:

```
>>> if "New York City FC" in mlsteams.values():
...     print "going to support NYC FC in MLS this year"
... else:
...     print "going to stick to NFL this year I guess"
...
```

going to support NYC FC in MLS this year

Nesting Dictionaries

It might look a little confusing at the start, but give it time and process it slowly. You will eventually see that it's not toocomplex. Here's how you can nest dictionaries.

```
>>> mlsteamsselect = {
... "Washington DC": {
...     "team": "DC United",
...     "joined": 1996
...     },
... "Bridgeview IL": {
...     "team": "Chicago Fire",
...     "joined": 1998
...     },
... "Toronto ON": {
...     "team": "Toronto FC",
...     "joined": 2007
...     }
... }
```

Our nested dictionaries aren't complicated, so retrieving data doesn't pose a serious challenge. After all, we already know the keys.

```
>>> mlsteamsselect["Toronto ON"]["team"]
```
'Toronto FC'

Please note that retrieving values from nested dictionaries, especially if they are dynamically updated and the keys can change, is very complex. We are going to avoid such an issue right now.

Tuples

As mentioned earlier, Python has borrowed a lot of concepts from mathematics. In simple terms, a tuple is an immutable version of lists. You can identify that tuple items are enclosed in parentheses. All the methods and functions that are applicable on a list also apply on tuples, except for the ones that add or remove list items.

Here's our first tuple:

```
>>> tuplenew = (1,"apple",1,"day","keeps the doctor away")
>>> tuplenew
```
(1, 'apple', 1, 'day', 'keeps the doctor away')

The only new trick to learn here is that there's a way to change items in a tuple. We change the tuple into a list, update items, and transform the list back to a tuple.

```
>>> listnew = list(tuplenew)
>>> listnew.pop(0)
1
>>> listnew.insert(0,"one")
>>> tuplenew = tuple(listnew)
>>> tuplenew
```
('one', 'apple', 1, 'day', 'keeps the doctor away')

Bonus: Sets

Sets contain items in an unindexed and unordered way. They are enclosed in curly brackets, which are also called braces. Be careful as sets look very similar to a dictionary, even though they are completely different. There are no keys in sets. Here's a simple set.

```
>>> veggies
set(['asparagus', 'broccoli', 'okra'])
```
You cannot change items in a set, but you can add new items or remove existing ones.

```
>>> veggies.add("beet")
>>> veggies
set(['asparagus', 'beet', 'broccoli', 'okra'])
```
Here's an example of adding multiple items using update():

```
>>> veggies.update(["eggplant","peas","corn"])
>>> veggies
set(['okra', 'asparagus', 'corn', 'peas', 'eggplant', 'broccoli'])
```

Bonus: Try veggies.update("potato","spinach") and check the contents of the veggies set.

To remove an item, we can use remove() method.

```
>>> veggies.remove("broccoli")
>>> veggies
set(['okra', 'asparagus', 'corn', 'peas', 'eggplant'])
```

This works like a charm, but there's a problem with remove() method. If the element to be removed by remove() is not found in the set, it results in an error. To avoid that, there's a discard() method for sets, too.

```
>>> veggies.discard("peas")
>>> veggies
set(['okra', 'asparagus', 'corn', 'eggplant'])
```

When using discard() to remove an element, no error is raised if the element is not present in the set.

Functions

In Python, you can name a code block and call it later with its name for execution. The code block might work on data that you can pass to the function during the call. These data points are known as the parameters of that function. You can have the function return the result of the work done or not, depending on your needs.

Let's create our first function. Here's a trick question for you: Can we use len() to count the number of digits in an integer value? The answer is no. Is there a way to do it? Yes, there are multiple ways to do it, some strain resources more than others. We are going to write a function that determines the length of an integer through a very basic technique.

```
>>> def cntint(num):
...     count = 0
...     while (num>0):
...             count = count + 1
...             num = num//10
...     return count
...
```

The def keyword is used to tell Python that we are writing a function.

We can use any name as the function name; it has the same naming convention as variable names. Our function will be receiving one input; that's why only one parameter num declared. When the while loop stops execution, the variable count will contain the number of digits in the integer that will be passed to the function. Let's test our function.

```
>>> cntint(549684)
6
Let's do one more experiment.
>>> testint = 9751
>>> cntint(testint)
4
```

It means that we can pass a variable to a function, and that variable value will be used as the function parameter. Now, let's create a function that uses two parameters. The new function will output the multiplication table of a number up to the times that we want.

```
>>> def mult_table(num,times):
...     for i in range(1,times+1):
...             print num,"x",i,"=",num*i
...
>>> mult_table(8,10)
8 x 1 = 8
8 x 2 = 16
8 x 3 = 24
8 x 4 = 32
8 x 5 = 40
8 x 6 = 48
8 x 7 = 56
8 x 8 = 64
8 x 9 = 72
8 x 10 = 80
```

Let's do something fun.

```
>>> mult_table("eight",10)
```
eight x 1 = eight

eight x 2 = eighteight

eight x 3 = eighteighteight

eight x 4 = eighteighteighteight

eight x 5 = eighteighteighteighteight

eight x 6 = eighteighteighteighteighteight

eight x 7 = eighteighteighteighteighteighteight

eight x 8 = eighteighteighteighteighteighteighteight

eight x 9 = eighteighteighteighteighteighteighteighteight

eight x 10 = eighteighteighteighteighteighteighteighteighteight

That actually worked! It goes to show that multiplication can be applied on a string.

This is intriguing. Let's create another function.

```
>>> def sum_var(num1,num2):
...     print num1+num2
...
>>> sum_var(1237,"all good?")
Traceback (most recent call last):
  File "<interactive input>", line 1, in <module>
  File "<interactive input>", line 2, in sum_var
TypeError: unsupported operand type(s) for +: 'int' and 'str'
```

All is not good apparently! This highlights the fact that it is important to create exception handling when writing functions because there can be a data type mismatch resulting in an execution breaking error. Exception handling is a technique used to take care of situations when an error can occur. In case an error happens, execution doesn't stop, and you can change the execution flow to follow an alternate approach.

The Concept of Recursion

In most programming languages, including Python, a function is allowed to call itself. This technique is quite useful in certain situations. However, utmost caution should be observed since recursion can lead to an infinite loop if it's not implemented properly. That can result in a system crash or at least in Python process becoming unresponsive.

Classes

Classes are used in Python to create objects. In real life, when you have to construct an object, you create a blueprint. Class fulfills the same purpose for creating objects in Python. Let's create our first class.

```
>>> class firstclass:
...     x = 789
...
```

The variable x is called a class property. Now, using the class, we can create new objects.

```
>>> obj1 = firstclass()
>>> obj1.x
789
```

As you can see, the property of the class has become a method of the object created with it. We can add function as a property to the class. In fact, there's a function __init__() that must be a part of every class you create. It is used to initialize a class so that it can be used to declare class properties and values or any dependencies.

Have you ever played a video game? In most video games, there are non-player characters that are only controlled by the computer. They can have any purpose according to the requirements of the game. Let's create a class for non-player character.

```
>>> class npcprofile:
...     def __init__(instance,type,name,hp,shield,specialmoves):
...             instance.type = type
...             instance.name = name
...             instance.hp = hp
...             instance.shield = shield
...             instance.specialmoves = specialmoves
...
```

The first property instance in the __init__() is used to denote the title which Python will use to internally call each object created with the npcprofile class. When passing data, remember not to pass any data for the first parameter.

Now, let us use the class to create a foot soldier object.

```
>>> npc1 = npcprofile("Grunt","Foot Soldier",50,0,[])
```

You can check all the values very easily.

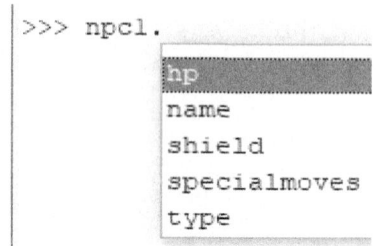

```
>>> npc1.
          hp
          name
          shield
          specialmoves
          type
```

Let's create a final level boss object.

```
>>> npc2 = npcprofile("Final Level Boss","General X",500,500,[5,"Hammer
Deagle","Double Trouble AK47","Nevermiss Dragunov","Stunning
Grenade","Rapidfire RPG"])
```

This boss is going to take some time to get beaten, for sure.

If you want to update any object property, you can do something like the example below.

```
>>> playerattack = 75
>>> if playerattack > 50:
...     npc1.hp = 0
...
>>> npc1.hp
0
```

You can use the del command to delete entire objects or a specific property.

```
>>> del npc1.specialmoves
>>> >>> del npc2
```

Working with Libraries

As mentioned many times in the book already, Python can be extended to meet specific project requirements. To highlight this point, we are going to work with an external library matplotlib which enables you to create 2D line charts (also called graphs or plots) using Python.

Here's an advantage of choosing PythonWin: it is pre-packaged with the matplotlib library. If we had chosen another Python environment, we would have to install matplotlib library with the help of pip. Since matplotlib is an external library, it's not loaded when Python starts. We have to import it before we can use it. Here is how to do that:

```
import matplotlib.pyplot as plt
```

When you import something, Python searches for it in the paths registered in its system. If you want to know which paths Python searches for looking for the library or module, here's the code:

```
>>> import sys
>>> for eachpath in sys.path:
...     print(eachpath)
...
```

You'll get a bunch of paths. If you are creating your own scripts, place them in one of these paths so that it'll be easier to import them. Still, it's not necessary as we'll see later.

Keep in mind that the process might take a while. If your Python screen becomes unresponsive, don't force-close it. Instead, give it a minute to return to normal. For our example, we are only calling the pyplot collection of functions from the matplotlib library. These functions can be used to plot a graph and change various parts of the graph.

Let's plot our first graph.

```
>>> plt.plot([1,2,3,4])
[<matplotlib.lines.Line2D object at 0x000000000B1DFEB8>]
```

The output confirms that the plot has been created, as well as where it's residing in the memory. Right now, the plot is hidden. We can make changes to the graph before we tell Python to show us the graph.

```
>>> plt.ylabel("Some numbers")
Text(0,0.5,u'Some numbers')
>>> plt.xlabel("Some numbers")
Text(0.5,0,u'Some numbers')
```

The outputs confirm that the labels for the x and y axes have been updated. Let's take a look at the plot.

```
>>> plt.show()
```

A new, small window will pop up on your screen showing the plot. It should look like this:

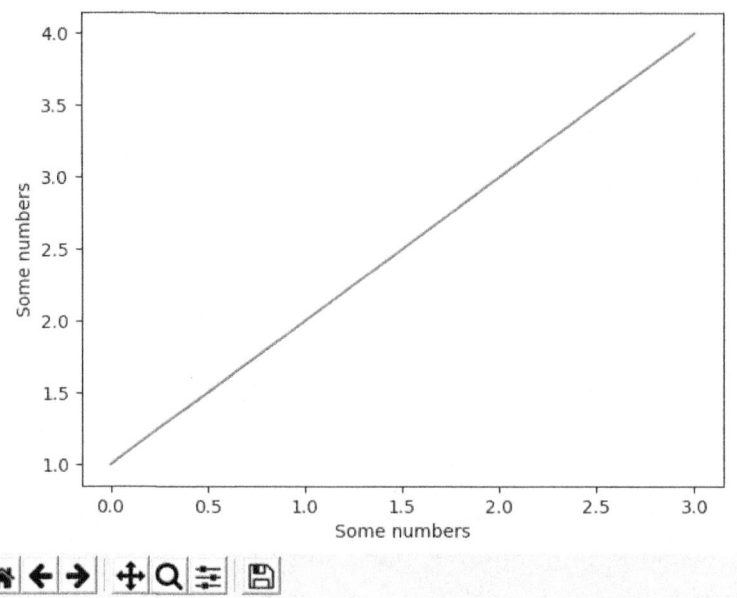

At the bottom-left corner of the window, you can see a row of buttons, each offering different functionality. You can resize the window if you want to look at a bigger plot. You can also see the custom labels we set for the x and y axes.

It was a simple straight line plot. We can create different types of 2D plots. We can also customize the look of the plot. Let's look at another example:

```
>>> plt.plot([1,2,3,4],'ro')
>>> plt.ylabel("Some numbers")
>>> plt.xlabel("Some numbers")
>>> plt.show()
```

Here's the output:

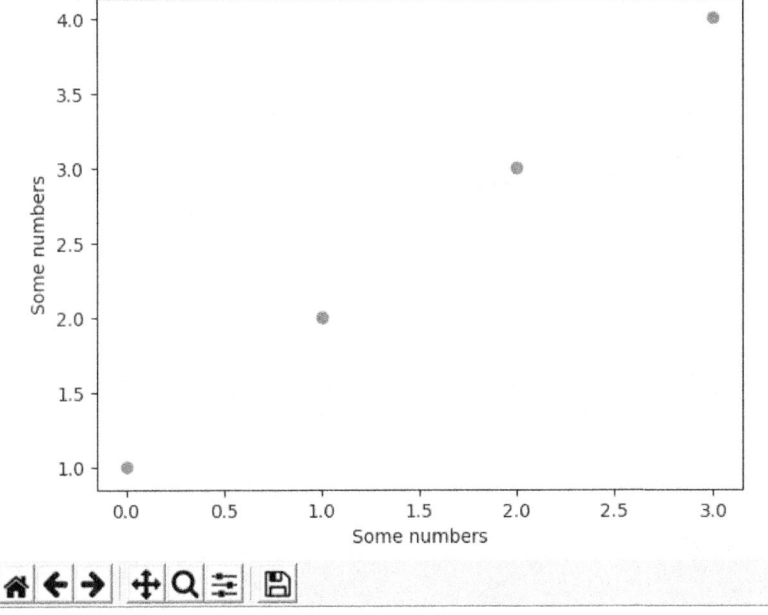

It's the same plot but instead of a solid blue line, we are seeing four red dots because we added the optional string '-ro'. The default is the string '-b' which is for the solid blue line. We can control the axes limits with the following statement.

```
plt.axis([0, 6, 0, 20])
```

The first two numbers are for x-axis and the last two for y-axis. Let's create a script, add following line of codes, and save it with the name firstplot.py.

```
import matplotlib.pyplot as plt
plt.plot([1,2,3,4], [1,4,9,16], 'ro')
plt.axis([0, 6, 0, 20])
plt.show()
```

Let's run the script. If you saved the file in the folder where Python is saved, you can run the script like this.

```
>>> import firstplot
```

To conserve resources, Python only runs import once for each entity. Subsequent runs of the command import firstplot will do nothing. We have an alternative: in Python 2.7, you can use the execfile() function to run any file as long as you have it's complete path. This is also useful if you are saving your scripts in a folder other than where Python is installed. One advantage that execfile() gives us is that we can use it as many times as we want to run our script. For example, let's grab the file path from Windows.

D:\Python27\myScripts

Name

firstplot.py

We see that the path of our file is D:\Python27\myScripts\. You will use execfile like this.

```
>>> execfile('D:/Python27/myScripts/firstplot.py')
```

Note how all the backward slashes in the path you got from Windows were replaced by forward slashes because execfile() doesn't recognize backward slashes in a file path.

As soon as you run the script, the plot will appear on your screen and should look like this:

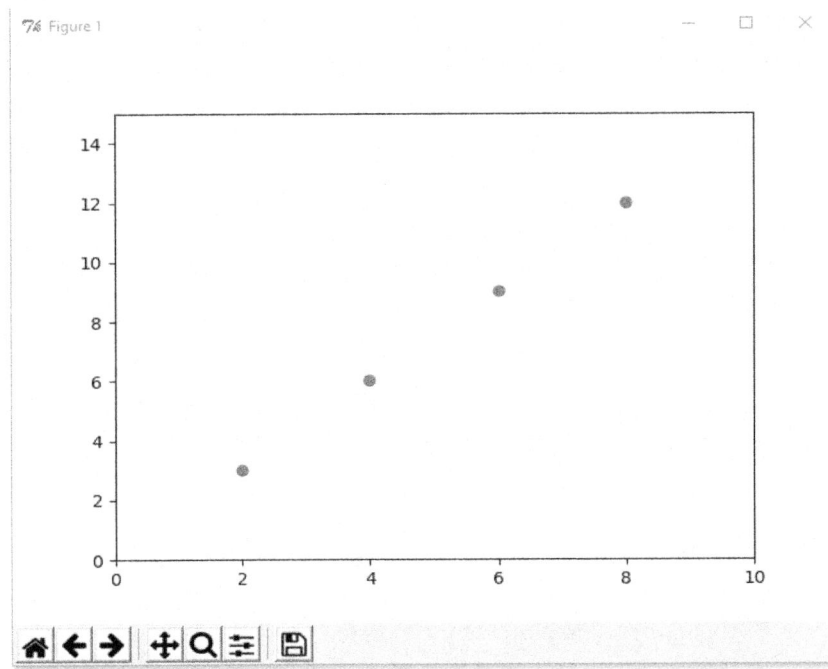

As long as this graph is visible, you won't be abl e to do anything in the interactive mode.

The matplotlib offers too many functionalities for plotting different data that it's impossible to cover here. We used this example to show how we can import an external library into Python and work with it. At this stage, you may be wondering if we can release imported libraries from memory to free up some resources. As mentioned earlier in the case of variables, Python automatically manages resources to deliver optimum performance. As soon as Python recognizes that it doesn't need to allocate resources to an external resource, it'll do as such. There are certain techniques to force-remove objects from memory and caches, but it's highly unrecommended.

Debugging

Debugging is the process of fixing any errors that happens during program execution. Python outputs a traceback, which is its way of producing all the details about the error to help you find and fix it. It can contain the line number and the type of error that has taken place. Python also highlights the position where it has encountered the issue with a caret sign.

In case you have made multiple errors, Python stops at the first error it stumbles upon, stops execution, and outputs the traceback. This is one of the biggest differences between an interpreter and a compiler language. In a compiler language like C, if you make multiple errors, you get an error report detailing all the errors. Sometimes, it can be too overwhelming, especially for new programmers.

Types of Errors in Python

In Python, errors are broadly classified into two types.

Syntax Errors

Sometimes called parsing errors, syntax errors happen if you add an extra string or character or forget to add the required ones.

We have encountered syntax error before. Let's recreate a situation that leads to a syntax error. Enter the following line of code in the Interactive Mode.

```
>>> for i in range(0,11):
...     print "This will produce a syntax error
```

As soon as you press Enter, you will see Python produce the following:

```
...     print "This will produce a syntax error
Traceback ( File "<interactive input>", line 2
    print "This will produce a syntax error
                                          ^
SyntaxError: EOL while scanning string literal
```

We missed the right quotation mark, which led to the syntax error.

Index Error

If you try to access information from a collection data structure with an index that doesn't have any data, you will get an index error. Here's an example:

```
>>> list1 = ["python","is","cool"]
>>> list1[5]
Traceback (most recent call last):
  File "<interactive input>", line 1, in <module>
IndexError: list index out of range
```

Type Error

This happens if you do an operation on data that they don't work with. For example, try to add an integer and a string.

```
>>> int1 = 143
>>> str1 + int1
>>> str1 + int1
Traceback (most recent call last):
  File "<interactive input>", line 1, in <module>
TypeError: cannot concatenate 'str' and 'int' objects
```

Fun fact: If you do int1 + str1, you will also get a type error, but the explanation will be a little different.

```
>>> int1 + str1
Traceback (most recent call last):
  File "<interactive input>", line 1, in <module>
TypeError: unsupported operand type(s) for +: 'int' and 'str'
```

Name Error

If you use an object that you didn't assign or declare a value beforehand, Python will throw a name error.

```
>>> list1 = ['python', 'is', 'cool']
>>> list2
Traceback (most recent call last):
  File "<interactive input>", line 1, in <module>
NameError: name 'list2' is not defined
```

Import Error

You will see this error if you try to import something and Python isn't able to find. Remember that Python only searches in the file paths registered with it.

```
>>> import myownmodule
Traceback (most recent call last):
  File "<interactive input>", line 1, in <module>
ImportError: No module named myownmodule
>>> from math import triangle
Traceback (most recent call last):
  File "<interactive input>", line 1, in <module>
ImportError: cannot import name triangle
```

Again, same error but two different descriptions.

There are many other exceptions in Python, but we are going to limit our discussion to the types mentioned above.

Logical Error

This error takes place when your problem-solving logic is flawed. This is the most difficult to find and fix because everything is fine for Python. There will be no syntax errors or exceptions, but the output will not be what you had expected. Program execution will not stop; there will be no traceback detailing the error either. You will be on your own. Scary, isn't it?

Let's look at an example where a logical error is happening. We are going to program the equation but consciously make a logical error to illustrate a point. Here's the equation we are coding: $y = \dfrac{x}{2\pi}$

```
import math
x = 100
y = x / 2 * math.pi
print y
```

When you save and run the script, you will get:

157.079632679

This is not the correct result. If you use a calculator, the result should have been 15.91 with a value of 100 for x. Meaning, there's something wrong with our script, but Python didn't find it.

The reason here is that we made a logical error. If you look at the expression y = x / 2 * math.pi closely, you will notice that Python is following PEDMAS. It means that if there are multiple operators with the same priority, Python will work from left to right. It's dividing x by 2 and then multiplying the quotient by the pi value. The correct way is that 2 should be multiplied with pi before x gets divided by their product.

To fix this logical error, you should update the expression with parentheses like below. Save the script and do a rerun.

```
y = x / ( 2 * math.pi )
```
Now, you should see the correct result:
```
15.9154943092
```

Exceptional Handling

Except when a syntax error occurs, you can code to handle all situations that might result in an error. Here's how we can do that.

```
>>> try:
...     print(varint)
... except:
...     print "An exception has occured!"
...
An exception has occured!
```

The code block inside "try" is tested for an exception. If one happens, the code block inside the "except" is executed. In this case, varint wasn't assigned a value, so it resulted in an exception that led to the execution of the code inside "except".

If you want to execute code if no exception is raised, use "else" (as seen below).

```
>>> varint = 100
>>> try:
...     print(varint)
... except:
...     print "An exception has occured!"
... else:
...     print(varint)
...
100
```

100

This time around, we have assigned a value to varint. Notice that the code block inside the "try" also gets executed in case there's no exception. This is why we see two output lines.

We can execute code irrespective of whether an exception is raised or not by the code block in "try" as well. We can use "finally" for that.

```
>>> x = "I am assigned"
>>> try:
...     print x
... except:
...     print "An exception has occured!"
... finally:
...     print "Hurray! No exception occured."
...
```

I am assigned

Hurray! No exception occured.

Best Debugging Practices

All the error examples we saw are pretty straightforward and easy to fix. However, as you will advance towards creating more complex programming techniques, you should know that debugging errors will become more challenging. It is a good idea to learn the best practices to avoid making errors and resolve them if you end up making some.

Algorithms and Flowcharts

Before you start programming, always write an algorithm. This helps you think about the task, the requirements, and the problem-solving process. This is the stage where you should be optimizing your approach. Once you start coding, it will be difficult to change your approach, and you might make more mistakes. Creating a flowchart helps you determine the dependencies of your solution.

Commentation

You should add comments to your code because you may forget what or why you did something specific. This helps in catching bugs later on or if you decide to optimize your code. It also makes your code derivable so that it will be easier for another person to use or build upon it in the future.

Dry Run

This is actually something that many modern programmers don't do. It is perhaps because of the modern debugging tools available now or because people have stopped handwriting most stuff. This is a tradition of running the code on a piece of paper. You go through your code line by line like an interpreter and right down all the updates. This is also a good way of catching bugs but may not be feasible if your program has hundreds of lines of code.

Test Unexpected Behavior

If you are creating a solution that other people will use, you should test your program with unexpected inputs. For example, if your program is expecting user to input an integer, there's a chance that the user might enter a float or even a string. Either can break your code if it doesn't have proper exception handling.

Debugging Tools

Python has a standard debugging tool pdb that you can use for your program. There are also external tools available out there in case you are looking for more options. We will briefly look into the pdb debugging tool, but let's update our firstplot.py script first.

```
import matplotlib.pyplot as plt, pdb
pdb.set_trace()
plt.plot([2,4,6,8], [3,6,9,12], 'ro')
plt.axis([0, 10, 0, 15])
plt.show()
```

The line where pdb.set_trace() is placed is where Python pdb debugger will start tracing. When you run the script now, you'll see a small window popping up along with some information on the

Interactive Window.

```
-> plt.plot([2,4,6,8], [3,6,9,12], 'ro')
```

This small window is where you can pass commands to the pdb debugger. Here is a list of some pdb commands that you can use to debug your script.

1. (s)tep - execute the line where debugger is currently at
2. (c)ontinue - execute until a breakpoint is encountered (It'll execute to the end of script if no breakpoint is found.)
3. (n)ext - execute until the start of next line in a function or until the function returns

Use "n" in the popup to keep executing each line in your script. It'll execute each line and show the next line.

Exercises

1. Write a program that takes input user's name and displays it 10 times on the screen.
2. Write a program that takes string input from the user and counts the number of spaces in it.
3. Write a program that takes the user's state as input and returns the zip code range for that state. You can easily find the zip code ranges for every US state on the internet.
4. Write a program that outputs all the prime numbers between the number range inputted by the user.

Write a program that gets three numbers as input from user and outputs the largest number.

CHAPTER FOUR

INTEGRATION WITH PYTHON

I n this chapter, we will briefly look into Python's capabilities to interact with completely different systems. Our goal is to showcase Python's flexibility. From here on, you should start placing codes within files and executing them because some of them might not work as expected in Python interpreter's Interactive Window.

Integration With OS: Windows

Get File Path

You can very easily get the file path where the python file is currently residing. It takes only two lines of code (as third line is just the output).

```
import os,sys
pathname=os.path.dirname(sys.argv[0])
print pathname
```

If you try to execute this code in Interactive Window, you'll see an empty output. Place the lines in a file and then save and run it to view the correct output. The output path will not contain the actual filename. We have imported two standard libraries "os" and "sys" that help us interact with most Windows functions. This is another advantage of picking PythonWin for coding Python on Windows.

Working With a Text File

Let's create a text file with Python and write "Hello, Universe!" in it.

```
import os,sys

a=os.path.dirname(sys.argv[0])
link=os.path.join(a,"firstfile.txt")
text=open(link,'w')
text.write("Hello, Universe!")
text.close()
```

The last line saves the file and is very necessary; otherwise, the file will remain open in the background. Now, if we want to read to file, we can do so as follows:

```
text=open(link,'r')
filetext = str(text.read())
print filetext
text.close()
```

The "r" and "w" arguments in open() tell Python if we want to open, file, read, or write data. We can also delete the file with a single line of code:

```
os.remove(link)
```

If the file is open, you'll get an error. You won't be able to delete the file before closing it.

Integration with MS Office

It's even easier to interact with applications running on Windows. In this chapter, we are going to take advantage of the Windows applications COM system that helps interacting with Windows application easily.

Working with Excel Files

As an example, for MS Office, we are going to create an MS Excel workbook, rename the sheet, put some data on it, save the file, and exit.

```
import os, sys
import win32com.client as win32

pathname=os.path.dirname(sys.argv[0])
excel=win32.gencache.EnsureDispatch('Excel.Application')
excel.Visible=True
wb=excel.Workbooks.Add()
ws=wb.Worksheets('Sheet1')
ws.Name='Python Created'
ws.Cells(1, 1).Value = "With"
ws.Cells(1, 2).Value = "Python"
ws.Cells(1, 3).Value = "2.7"
```

raw_input() # This is only to hold the screen so you can see the excel file. You don't need to even enter anything, just click on OK and program execution will continue

```
filename = os.path.join(pathname,'firstexcelfile.xlsx')
wb.SaveAs(filename,win32.constants.xlOpenXMLWorkbook)          #saving
workbook
excel.Application.Quit()
```

This will place an Excel file in the same folder where you will save the script file. The win32com.client enables Python to interact with and take control of Windows applications. This is exclusively available with PythonWin. The expression excel.Visible=True keeps the excel workbook visible; otherwise, everything will run in the background.

Integration with Java

You can run Java codes within Python with the help of Py4J external library. For starters, install the library with pip. Note that you'll need Java installed on your system, too.

```
python -m pip install py4j
```

Our purpose isn't to learn Java in this book, so we are going to look at an example of Java code here that we'll later run in Python.

```java
import py4j.GatewayServer;

public class AdditionApplication {

  public int addition(int first, int second) {
      return first + second;
  }

  public static void main(String[] args) {
      AdditionApplication app = new AdditionApplication();
      // app is now the gateway.entry_point
      GatewayServer server = new GatewayServer(app);
      server.start();
  }
}
```

Python will run the Java code and get variable values to print the output. To run the above code in Python, here's the Python code:

```python
from py4j.java_gateway import JavaGateway
gateway = JavaGateway()                  # connect to the JVM
random = gateway.jvm.java.util.Random()  # create a java.util.Random instance
number1 = random.nextInt(10)             # call the Random.nextInt method
number2 = random.nextInt(10)
print(number1, number2)
addition_app = gateway.entry_point           # get the AdditionApplication instance
value = addition_app.addition(number1, number2)) # call the addition method
print(value)
```

In the second line gateway = JavaGateway(), the comment says "connect with JVM", not "start JVM". This is an important point. Py4J doesn't have the capabilities to start JVM, so you must do it yourself before using Python to run Java codes.

Integration with MySQL and MS Access

Working with MySQL

MySQL is the most popular database framework for small- and medium-scale applications. To work with MySQL with Python, we have to install the external library mysql-connecter using the pip.

```
python -m pip install mysql-connector
```

Once installed, we can start working with a database.

```
import mysql.connector as mysql

myfirstdb = mysql.connect(
  host="localhost",
  user="yourusername",
  passwd="yourpassword"
)

print(myfirstdb)
```

For the "yourusername" and "yourpassword", you need to enter the username and password that you like for the database. The print statement should output an object, confirming that a database connection has been established.

Password Generation

You can use Python to create secure MD5 hash passwords. By using MD5 hashing, you can convert a string called key into a hash of characters that you can use as a password. As long as you keep the key safe, it's almost impossible to crack a MD5 password. Here's the code to get a string input from user and generate a password with it:

```
import hashlib

getkey = raw_input("Enter your key to generate MD5 password: ")
print hashlib.md5(getkey).hexdigest()
```

We have used the hashlib library that gives us the capability to generate a MD5 hash.

Create a Database

To create database, we have to create a cursor instance that will allow us to execute SQL commands on our database.

```
cursor = myfirstdb.cursor()
cursor.execute("CREATE DATABASE myfirstdb")
```

If you want to see the list of databases present in the system, use the following lines of code:

```
databaselist = cursor.fetchall()
print databaselist #print the complete list of databases
```

```
# if you want to output each database separately
for database in databaselist:
        print database
```

Create Tables

Database is a collection of data tables. If we don't create any tables, there's no purpose for a database. Let's connect to one that we created and add a table to it.

```
db = mysql.connect(
      host = "localhost",
      user = "yourusername",
      passwd = "yourpassword",
      database = "myfirstdb"
)
cursor = db.cursor()

cursor.execute("CREATE TABLE users (name VARCHAR(255), user_name
VARCHAR(255))")
```

Now, let's create a primary key that will help access each row uniquely, as well as add data to the table.

```
cursor.execute("CREATE TABLE users (id INT(11) NOT NULL
AUTO_INCREMENT PRIMARY KEY, name VARCHAR(255), user_name
VARCHAR(255))") # create primary key to access each row

query = "INSERT INTO users (name, user_name) VALUES (%s, %s)"
values = ("Anthony", "Martial")
cursor.execute(query, values)
db.commit()
```

There are many things you can do with a database using Python.

Working With MS Access

If you work extensively with MS Office product suite, you may use MS Access for your projects. Just like MS Excel, it is very easy to connect and manage a MS Access database using Python.

Here's a sample code that connects to MS Access database named "DATA_DUMP.mdb". The code accesses the database table "A_BTS" and selects the cell values in columns "bscId", "bcdId", and "btsId" where the column cell ID has value "65213".

```
import os, sys
import win32com.client as win32

conn = win32.Dispatch("ADODB.Connection")
pathname=os.path.dirname(sys.argv[0])
filename=os.path.join(pathname,"DATA_DUMP.mdb")
db = r"%s"%filename
DSN="Driver={Microsoft Access Driver (*.mdb)};DBQ=" + db
```

```
conn.Open(DSN)

rs = win32.Dispatch("ADODB.Recordset")
rs.Open( "A_BTS", conn, 1, 3 )

cmd = win32.Dispatch("ADODB.Command")
cmd.ActiveConnection = conn
cell="65213"
cmd.CommandText = "SELECT bscId,bcfId,btsId FROM A_BTS WHERE
cellId=%s;"%cell

(rs, result) = cmd.Execute()
```

Exercises

1. What is an operating system? Name a few famous operating systems.

2. Is MS Office the only software suite that provides spreadsheet and word-processing applications? Can you think of any alternatives?

3. Besides MySQL and MS Access, are there any other platforms that deal with database management?

4. Take a number input from user and create a multiplication table of that up to times 10 and output the table in a text file.

5. Copy the text file you just created to the desktop of your computer.

Find any text files in the folder where the script is and add a random number between 1000 and 9999 at the end of their filename. For example, multiplicationtable.txt should become multiplicationtable_randomnumber.txt.

CHAPTER FIVE

WORKING WITH FILES

We have already explored some of the options in the last chapter. Now, we are going to look into advanced techniques for Excel, PDF, and Word files.

Excel Spreadsheets

MS Excel is arguably the most popular spreadsheet software in the world. Not only you can perform advanced statistical analysis, but you can also automate everything with the help of macro recording. If you know Visual Basic, you can customize the macros to gain even more advantage. If you know Python, though, you don't need macros or Visual Basic.

Opening and Closing Spreadsheets

We have already seen how we can open an MS Excel file if we already know the file path. We want to enable the user to browse their computer and select the file that we should use in our program. To make it happen, we are going to briefly look into the Python's standard library for GUI, the Tkinter. This may be a difficult name to pronounce, but it is extremely powerful in providing GUI services to Python programmers.

Here's the code that'll enable the user to select a file. Then, we can get the file path from it.

```
import Tkinter,tkFileDialog

root = Tkinter.Tk()
root.withdraw() #use to hide tkinter window
file = tkFileDialog.askopenfile(parent=root,initialdir="/",mode='rb',title='Choose a file')
if file != None:
    print file.name
```

If we want to restrict the file type that the user can open, we can do so by adding type arguments to the tkFileDialog.askopenfile(). Modify that line for Excel files.

```
import Tkinter,tkFileDialog

root = Tkinter.Tk()
root.withdraw() #use to hide tkinter window
file = tkFileDialog.askopenfile(parent=root,initialdir="/",mode='rb',title='Choose a file',filetypes = (("All Excel files","*.xl*"),("All files","*.*")))
if file != None:
    print file.name
```

Parsing Data

To learn this topic, we are going to use the file that we have created while learning about MS Excel in the previous chapter. With the MS Excel file path, we can now open the file using the following command:

```
import win32com.client as win32

excel=win32.gencache.EnsureDispatch('Excel.Application')
excel.Visible=True
```

```
wb=excel.Workbooks.Open(file.name)
```

Alternate Approach

There are different ways to read the data on an Excel file, which is the first part of the process called data parsing. Broadly speaking, parsing is the analysis of data syntax. Since we are using PythonWin, we can use the available library "xlrd" to read the Excel file data. Here's a sample code to open an Excel file using "xlrd":

```
wb = xlrd.open_workbook(file.name)
```

When you use "xlrd", you might not be able to see the changes because the process is performed in the background. Also, you might have problems with ".xlsx" files. You can, however, combine both approaches to the previous one to view the Excel file and read the data.

Now, you can access the sheets in the file through either their name or index.

```
ws = workbook.sheet_by_name('Sheet1') # get sheet by title
ws = workbook.sheet_by_index(0) # get sheet by position
```

Using sheet titles is more reliable because you can change the position of sheets. To get the value of the first cell, use the following statement:

```
print ws.cell(0, 0).value
```

Note that the first cell of the excel for xlrd has row = 0 and column = 0. This is a bit different than when we used our approach in the previous chapter (where first cell had an index of row = 1 and column = 1). You can easily create a for loop to read all the data from the Excel file by building upon this method. One important thing to remember here is that if you try to use an index that doesn't have any set value, you'll get an error. For example, the following code will generate an index error:

```
print ws.cell(0,3).value
```

If you look at the file you created previously, the cell with position row = 0 and column = 3 doesn't have a set value. The above statement will result in an error.

The order traceback will look like this:

```
Traceback (most recent call last):
  File "D:\Python27\Lib\site-packages\PythonWin\pywin\framework\scriptutils.py",
line 326, in RunScript
    exec codeObject in __main__.__dict__
  File "D:\Python27\myScripts\openandparse.py", line 16, in <module>
    print ws.cell(0,50).value
  File "D:\Python27\lib\site-packages\xlrd\sheet.py", line 408, in cell
    self._cell_types[rowx][colx],
IndexError: array index out of range
```

To work around this, we can get the number of rows and columns in a sheet.

```
print "number of rows:",ws.nrows # get number of rows
print "number of columns:",ws.ncols # get number of columns
```

Modifying Spreadsheet Data

We can use another library "xlwt" to write data in the Excel file. We will have to install the library using pip.

```
python -m pip install xlwt
```

Writing data is a bit easier because you do not have to worry about any cell's row and column. We can use a for loop to update data on a spreadsheet. Here's a sample code:

```
import xlwt

wbw = xlwt.Workbook(encoding="utf-8")
wsw = wbw.add_sheet("Python Created")
wsw.write(0, 0, "Using xlwt to fill a cell")
wbw.save("D:/Python27/myScripts/chapter 5/secondexcelfile.xls")
```

The xlwt library has one limit, though, as it can only create MS Excel files with the older ".xls". Excel will recognize the file and open it but in compatibility mode. We can use some other library to create ".xlsx" files, such as xlsxwriter, or our initial method to read Excel files to create ".xlsx". Let's try the latter option to create an Excel file by assigning the header of "Index" to column A and populating column A with numbers 2 to 10.

```
import os, sys
import win32com.client as win32

#create data array
i = 2
data_array = []
while i < 11:
    data_array.append(i)
    i = i + 1

#write the array to an excel file
excel = win32.Dispatch("Excel.Application")
excel.Visible = True
wb = excel.Workbooks.Add()
ws = wb.Worksheets(1)

ws.Cells(1,1).Value = "Index" # create column header
#single loop, writing a column
for line in data_array:
    ws.Cells(line,1).Value = line

pathname=os.path.dirname(sys.argv[0])
filepath=os.path.join(pathname,"secondexcelfile.xlsx")
wb.SaveAs(filepath,win32.constants.xlOpenXMLWorkbook)

# cleaning up resources
ws = None
wb = None
excel.Quit()
excel = None
```

Working with PDF and Word Documents

Word Documents

Using PythonWin to work with MS Word is almost similar to using MS Excel. Here's the code that starts a MS Word process, creates a document, adds data to it, and saves it with the name "firstwordfile.docx" in the same folder where you would have saved this script.

```
import os, sys
import win32com.client as win32

word = win32.gencache.EnsureDispatch('Word.Application')
doc = word.Documents.Add()
```

```
word.Visible = True

RANGE = range(1, 11)
rng = doc.Range(0,0)
rng.InsertAfter('Python Created\r')
for i in RANGE:
        rng.InsertAfter('Line %d\r' % i)
        rng.InsertAfter("Hello, Universe!\r\r")


pathname=os.path.dirname(sys.argv[0])
filepath=os.path.join(pathname,"firstwordfile.docx")
doc.SaveAs(filepath)
word.Application.Quit()
```

Opening an existing Word document is easy. Here's the complete code:

```
import Tkinter,tkFileDialog
import win32com.client as win32
import os, sys


root = Tkinter.Tk()
root.withdraw() #use to hide tkinter window
file = tkFileDialog.askopenfile(parent=root,initialdir="/",mode='r',title='Choose a
file',filetypes = (("All Word files","*.doc*"),("All files","*.*")))
if file != None:
    print file.name


filepath_str = str(file.name)
filepath = filepath_str.replace("/","\\")
print type(filepath)
print filepath

word = win32.gencache.EnsureDispatch('Word.Application')
word.Visible = True

doc = word.Documents.Open(filepath)
doc.Activate()
docText = doc.Content

doc.Close(0)
word.Application.Quit()
```

To make things easier, we can install a library called python-docx using pip.

```
python -m pip install python-docx
```

Once installation is done, we can use it to read data from any Word document. Note that we can use this library for ".docx" Word files only.

```
import Tkinter,tkFileDialog
import docx

root = Tkinter.Tk()
root.withdraw() #use to hide tkinter window
file = tkFileDialog.askopenfile(parent=root,initialdir="/",mode='r',title='Choose a
file',filetypes = (("All Word files","*.doc*"),("All files","*.*")))
if file != None:
    print file.name


filepath_str = str(file.name)
filepath = filepath_str.replace("/","\\")
print type(filepath)
print filepath

doc = docx.Document(filepath)
print len(doc.paragraphs)
```

This will give you the number of paragraphs in the document. If you want to get all the text in a Word document, here's a sample code:

```
fullText = []
for para in doc.paragraphs:
fullText.append(para.text)
return '\n'.join(fullText)
```

You can also apply any style available in MS Word to any part of the document. For example, let's try the "Normal" style to the first paragraph.

```
doc.paragraphs[0].style = "Normal"
```

To get an individual sentence in a paragraph and apply a style to it, here's a code. Note that each sentence is referred to as a run.

```
doc.paragraphs[1].runs[0].underline = True
To save the changes in a new file, use this command:
doc.save("D:/Python27/myScripts/chapter 5/restyledfirstwordfile.docx")
```

You can also add an image to the end of the document with the following command:

```
doc.add_picture('filepath/image.png', width=docx.shared.Inches(1),
height=docx.shared.Cm(4))
```

Add the images' full file path in the first argument. The width and height arguments are optional, but you can use them to specify a certain size. If width and height aren't provided, the image will be added in the default size. Note that in Word, images are sized in physical units like inches (in) and centimeters (cm).

To add a page break, use this command:

```
doc.paragraphs[3].runs[3].add_break(docx.text.WD_BREAK.PAGE)
```
To create line breaks, you just have to add a new paragraph.
```
doc.add_paragraph('This is the next paragraph!')
```
You can also add a heading.
```
doc.add_heading('Title Heading', 0)
```
The first argument is the heading text while the other one defines the heading level which can go from 0 to 4.

PDF Documents

The Portable Document Format (PDF) documents are the undeclared standard of transmitting documents over the internet. There have been many changes to PDF documents over the years as they now support so much more features. To extract data from a PDF file, we are going to use an external library called PyPDF2. There are later versions of this library as well, such as PyPDF3 and PyPDF4. However, the only major difference in the later versions is their support for Python 3+ versions.

This library has one limitation: it only allows you to extract textual content from the PDF files. Sometimes, the library will fail to extract text from a PDF file or the extracted data might be corrupted.

Let's install the library.
```
python -m pip install PyPDF2
```
Once installed, we can start working with PDF files. Here is the code to get the number of pages in a PDF named "example.pdf":

import PyPDF2
```
import os, sys

pathname = os.path.dirname(sys.argv[0])
filepath = os.path.join(pathname,"example.pdf")
pdffile = open(filepath,'rb')
readpdf = PyPDF2.PdfFileReader(pdffile)
print readpdf.numPages
```
For me, the PDF file contained 2 pages, so I got the same output. We can extract the text content for a specific with the codes below.
```
pdfpage = readpdf.getPage(0)
pdfpage.extractText()
```
Note that the first page has an index 0. So, the last page will have an index readpdf.numPages - 1.

PDF files are sometimes encrypted. We can check if the file is encrypted with the following command:

```
readpdf.isEncrypted
```

If the output returned is true, you will not be able to extract text from the file. If you have the password — let's say it is "securedpdf" — you can decrypt the file.

```
readpdf.decrypt("securedpdf")
```

We can also use PyPDF2 to create PDFs. However, since you are not able to edit a PDF, you cannot add text or any media to this new PDF file. During creation, you can source content from other PDFs and performing page operations like rotation, overlay, and encryption.

```
import PyPDF2
import os, sys

pathname = os.path.dirname(sys.argv[0])
filepath = os.path.join(pathname,"example.pdf")
filepathnew = os.path.join(pathname,"examplenew.pdf")
pdffile = open(filepath,'rb')
readpdf = PyPDF2.PdfFileReader(pdffile)
writepdf = PyPDF2.PdfFileWriter()

for pagenum in range(0,readpdf.numPages):
    pdfpage = readpdf.getPage(pagenum)
    writepdf.addPage(pdfpage)

newpdf = open(filepathnew,'wb')
writepdf.write(newpdf)

newpdf.close()
pdffile.close()
```

The addPage() will only add new pages at the end of the document. You cannot insert pages in between others.

You can rotate after getting the page. As an example, let's rotate the first page by 90 degrees.

```
pdfpage = readpdf.getPage(0)
pdfpage.rotateClockwise(90)
```

PyPDF2 only allows you to rotate a page in 90 degree increments.

You can build upon the above codes to read pages and content from different PDF fields and merge them into a single PDF file.

Working With CSV and JSON Data

This is relatively easy. Python can work with Comma Separated Values (CSV) files and (JavaScript Object Notation) JSON files separately.

Interacting with CSV Files

There is a standard library in Python aptly named "csv" that enables programmers to open csv files and parse available data.

Let's add the following data in a csv file, name it "familynfriends_bday.csv", and save it in a folder where we will save the following code:

```
name,relation,birthday month
Samantha Sam,mother,November
Samuel Jones,father,August
Sasha Sam,sister,March
Samuel Jones Jr.,self,June
Here's the code to read the csv data:
import csv
import os, sys

pathname=os.path.dirname(sys.argv[0])
filepath = os.path.join(pathname,"familynfriends_bday.csv")

with open(filepath, mode='r') as csv_file:
    csv_reader = csv.DictReader(csv_file)
    line_count = 0
    for row in csv_reader:
        if line_count == 0:
            print 'Column names are',row.keys()
            line_count += 1
        print row['name'],"who is my",row['relation'],"has birthday in",row['birthday month']
        line_count += 1
    print 'Processed',line_count,"lines"
```

This will yield the following:

>>> Column names are ['birthday month', 'relation', 'name']

Samantha Sam who is my mother has birthday in November

Samuel Jones who is my father has birthday in August

Sasha Sam who is my sister has birthday in March

Samuel Jones Jr. who is my self has birthday in June

Processed 5 lines

Each row is read as a dictionary with the keys taken from the first row and the data from the relevant row. In a dictionary, the order is lost; that's why the column names don't appear in the first output line. In the sequence, they are present in the csv file.

To write a csv file, we can create a dictionary and pass the dictionary content to the csv file.

```
import csv
import os, sys

pathname=os.path.dirname(sys.argv[0])
filepath = os.path.join(pathname,"friends_bday.csv")

with open(filepath, mode='w') as csv_file:
    fieldnames = ['Friend Name', 'How long we have been friends?', 'Month']
    writer = csv.DictWriter(csv_file, fieldnames=fieldnames)

    writer.writeheader()
    writer.writerow({'Friend Name': 'John Smith', 'How long we have been friends?': '9 years', 'Month': 'November'})
    writer.writerow({'Friend Name': 'Erica Meyers', 'How long we have been friends?': '10 months', 'Month': 'January'})
```

Interacting With JSON Data

JSON has become the main technique of website data parsing. It evolved from the Javascript subset that deals with syntax of objects. With time, it has grown so much that it now how separately developed standards that are completely independent from Javascript.

Here's a sample of JSON data.

```
{
  "firstName": "Michel",
  "lastName": "Scott",
  "hobbies": ["mentoring", "godfather", "love"],
  "age": 40,
  "children": [
    {
      "firstName": "Sam the dog",
      "age": 6
    },
    {
      "firstName": "Bob the builder",
      "age": 8
    }
```

```
    ]
  }
```

Yes, it looks very much like a nested dictionary, but dealing with JSON cannot be that simple. Luckily, Python has a built-in library to read and write JSON.

```
import json

jsondata = '{"name": "Joshua", "age": 30, "city": "Boston"}'
pydata = json.loads(jsondata)
print pydata['name']
```

The JSON object was converted to a Python dictionary. The above code will produce "Joshua" when executed.

Whenever you convert JSON to Python or vice versa, data objects are converted to their equivalent counterpart. Here's a table that shows the conversion pattern.

Python	JSON
Dictionary	Object
List	Array
Tuple	Array
String	String
Integer	Number
Float	Number
True	true
False	false
None	null

To convert Python data to JSON, we can use the dumps() method. Refer to the following example.

```
import json
```

```
newpydata = {
    "name": "Trevor",
    "age": 29,
    "married": True,
    "orphan": False,
    "children": ["Suzie","Billy"],
    "pets": None,
    "cars": (
{"model": "Audi A7", "year": 2017},
{"model": "Dodge Caravan", "year": 2015}
)
}
newjsondata = json.dumps(newpydata)
print newjsondata
```

This will yield the newly converted JSON data that looks like this:

>>> {"name": "Trevor", "cars": [{"model": "Audi A7", "year": 2017}, {"model": "Dodge Caravan", "year": 2015}], "age": 29, "married": true, "orphan": false, "pets": null, "children": ["Suzie", "Billy"]}

It might be hard to read, but there are formatting options when using dumps() method. For example, we can add an indent for each line of data.

```
newjsondata = json.dumps(newpydata, indent=4)
```

We can also use custom separators and control the data sorting.

```
newjsondata = json.dumps(newpydata, indent=4, separators = (". ","," = "), sort_keys = True)
```

The output will now look similar to this:

```
>>> {
    "age" = 29.
    "cars" = [
        {
            "model" = "Audi A7".
            "year" = 2017
        }.
        {
            "model" = "Dodge Caravan".
            "year" = 2015
        }
    ].
    "children" = [
```

```
    "Suzie".
    "Billy"
  ].
  "married" = true.
  "name" = "Trevor".
  "orphan" = false.
  "pets" = null
}
```

Exercises

1. Create an ordered dictionary. Meaning, when you produce dictionary content, it should be in the same order that the key-value pairs were added to the dictionary.

2. From the user, take the following 10 inputs and create an Excel file and populate the first row with the titles below. Then, the second row should have the user inputs.
   a. First Name
   b. Last Name
   c. Age
   d. Zip code
   e. Education
   f. Driver? Yes/No
   g. Height
   h. Weight
   i. Time spent on cell phone
   j. Commute time to work

3. Add a new sheet in the Excel file created. Rename it as "Extra Sheet".

4. Reverse all the inputs you gathered from the user and add it to "Extra Sheet".

5. Save the excel file using the "Save As" option from Tkinter.

6. Create an Excel file with the extension ".xls" and add the prime numbers between 0 and 10,000. Use two columns of

the Excel file to produce the numbers.

7. Manually download the PDF file from the URL http://www.africau.edu/images/default/sample.pdf and read all the data.

8. Save all the data read from the PDF file to a MS Word document.

9. Take inputs from user, asking for 20 random numbers, and store in a csv file. Then, access the CSV file and find the largest number.

10. Convert the largest number to JSON data.

CHAPTER SIX

ADVANCED CONCEPTS

I f you think that we have been doing advanced work with Python, you will be surprised by this chapter. Let's hear it again: Python is a very powerful language! You can perform complex tasks and schedule them to achieve complete automation.

Scheduling Tasks

Task scheduling is relatively easy on a Windows system. You can use the "Task Scheduler" available by default on all Windows installations to arrange the execution of a Python script you have programmed.

Click on the Windows logo on the bottom-left side of your screen and search for "Task Scheduler". From the list, open the application with the same name. On Windows 10, the application will look this:

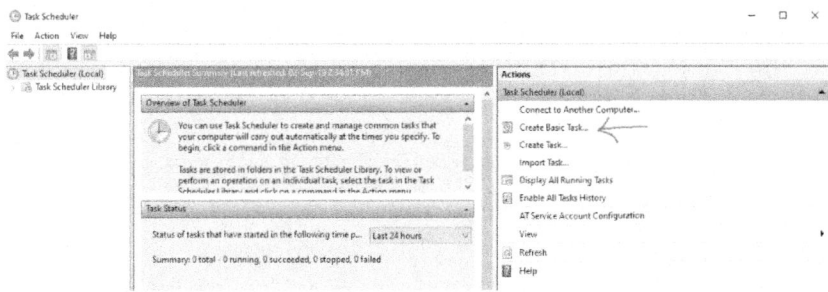

Click "Create Basic Task". A new window named "Create Basic Task Wizard" will pop up.

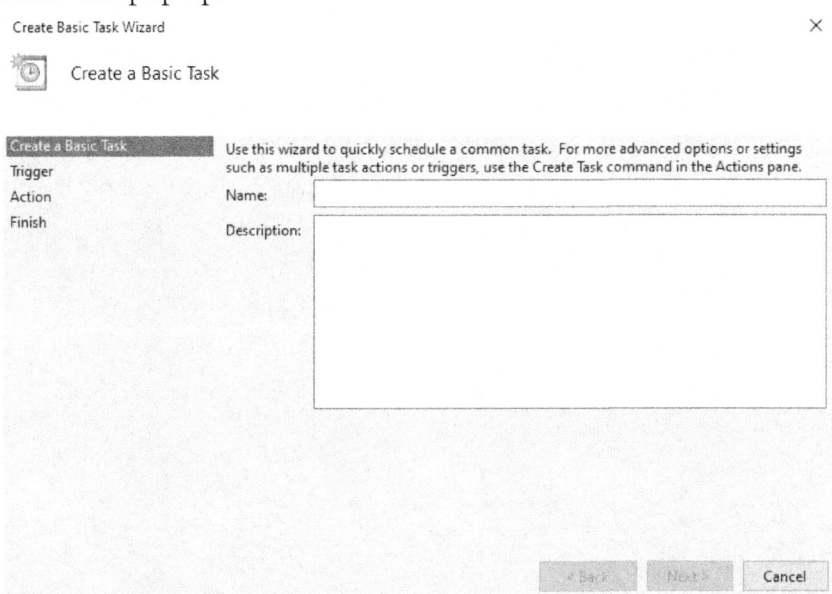

Here are short descriptions for your options:

1. Provide a name that you'll recognize easily later on. You can also provide a description to help you remember what the task's purpose is. Click "Next".

2. Now, you can select a trigger. It can be a specific time or event that happens in a Windows application or system. For our example, let's choose the first option "Daily".

3. Pick 6:29pm everyday and today's date as starting point. Keep one in the recur field. Click "Next".

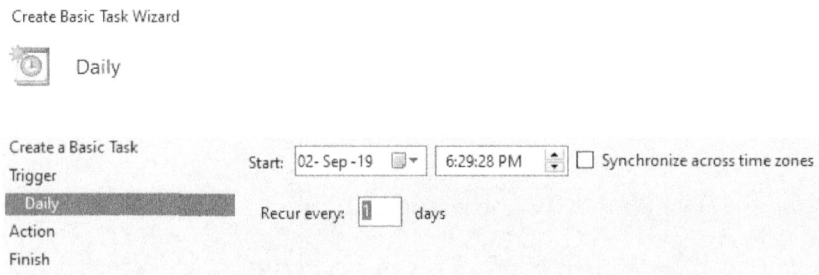

4. Now, we have to set an action that Windows should take when the trigger happens. We will keep the option "Start a program" selected because that's what we want to do. Click "Next".

5. Enter the parameters of the program we want to run. To execute a Python script, it's advisable to run the Python first and then pass the script as an argument. For example, if you want to schedule the script D:\myscript.py and the executable Python is located at C:\Python27\python.exe, here's how you should enter the details.

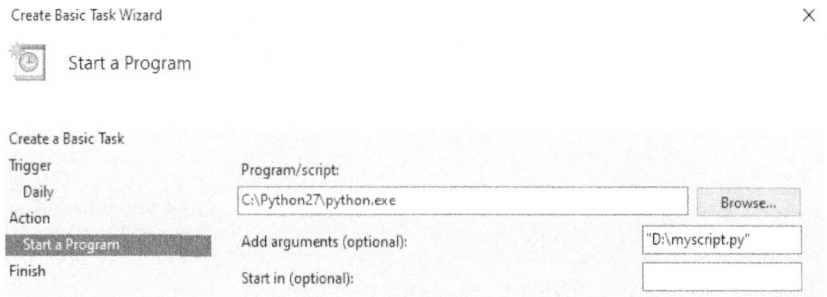

Now, when you click "Next", you will see a summary of the task.

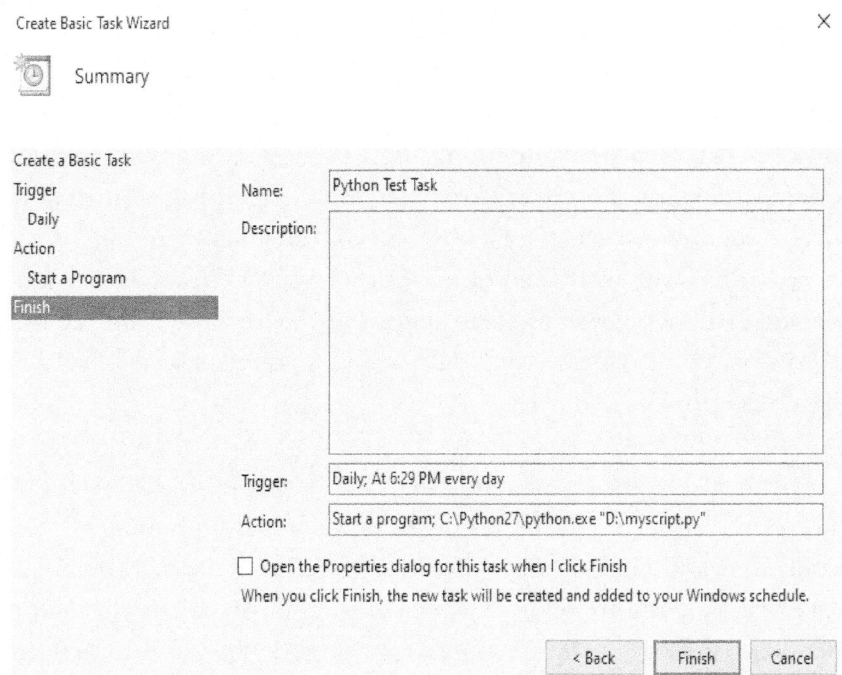

Click on "Finish" and the task will be scheduled.

This is a very nifty way to automate your daily activities.

Windows has Batch (.bat) files that are Windows script files. To schedule a task, an alternative approach is to create a batch file and schedule it using the Windows "Task Scheduler". In the batch file, we can add instructions to run the Python script. To schedule the execution of our D:\myscript.py file, we can add the following instruction to the batch file:

```
C:\Python27\python.exe "D:\myscript.py"
```

When we started with the Task Scheduler, we chose the "Create Basic Task" on the first screen. Below that, there was an option "Create Task" that offers advanced options to create the task.

Web Scraping

While learning about Python's package manager pip, we installed an external library called Scrapy. Before we jump into action, though, let's talk about web scraping.

In the last decade, data science has started to affect the life of every human being in the world. Everything is data. Every action you take online and sometimes even in real life are recorded by someone and processed to sell you something. If you have seen any tech industry documentary on Discovery or National Geographic, you may have heard the phrase "Data is now more valuable than oil." I don't necessarily agree with the notion, but it might be true. The point for debate is if people want their actions to be recorded and analyzed. With service providers doing data analysis online, it looks like there's no choice for the end user.

Nevertheless, data science also helps society and improves the lives of commoners. You can find numerous researches based on data collection and analysis that have led to better actions. It is already a fact that humans are habitual species, after all. By analyzing their past actions, you can form a pattern and predict their future actions in certain situations. What's the limit of that? That's up for debate.

The concept of web scraping is that anything you can or cannot see on a website can be scraped. Web scraping can be very beneficial for developing new products that require data that you don't have resources to collect. For example, you want to create a mobile application that tells farmers daily sunrise time and synchronize their alarms or maybe setup reminders.

In the near future, smart homes will become a reality. You may want to create an application that pulls the bedroom's curtains as the first sun rays come through the window! For this purpose, it's not possible to start collecting data about sun's movement yourself. The task will be much easier if you have access to a weather forecasting service or NASA's solar system data. If they post the relevant information on their website, you can write a script to crawl it on their website and extract the required pieces. On the other side of the spectrum, it's a very easy tool to steal copyrighted material from a website. This is why ethics is very important when it comes to data science and web scraping.

Let's start learning web scraping with Python.

As a first step, we need to setup a project using Scrapy. Open the command prompt — yes, the one you use to install Python libraries — and change directory to where you want the project files to reside using the cd command. After that, enter:

```
scrapy startproject myfirstspider
```

To scrape data from websites, we need to create a crawler. It is also called a spider because it crawls through the required areas of given website. Since this is our first scraping project, we have named it "myfirstspider". You can name it anything you like. In truth, you might want to, especially if you don't like spiders! After running the command, a folder will be created in the path that you had decided on before. In our case, the folder name is "myfirstspider" that resides in D:\Python27\myScripts\chapter 6\.

Now, we have to update the file \myfirstspider\myfirstspider\settings.py and create our customized spider inside the \myfirstspider\myfirstspider\spiders\ folder.

In the settings.py file, we have to make two changes. First, uncomment the ITEMS_PIPELINE tuple if it's commented out and edit it to look like this:

```
#Export as CSV Feed
FEED_FORMAT = "csv"
FEED_URI = "reddit.csv"
```

This is because we are going to save the scraped data in the reddit.csv file in the location D:\Python27\myScripts\chapter 6\ourfirstscraper\reddit.csv.

Now, in the command prompt, add the following command to create a customized spider inside the \myfirstspider\myfirstspider\spiders\ folder using a standard template:

```
scrapy genspider redditbot www.reddit.com/r/gameofthrones/
```

The new spider is named redditbot, and we will be scraping thread titles and image from the Games of Thrones Reddit page.

If you open the \myfirstspider\myfirstspider\spiders\redditbot.py file, you'll see the following:

```
import scrapy

class RedditbotSpider(scrapy.Spider):
    name = 'redditbot'
    allowed_domains = ['www.reddit.com/r/gameofthrones']
    start_urls = ['http://www.reddit.com/r/gameofthrones']

    def parse(self, response):
        pass
```

A few pointers:

1. We can give any name of the spider. For now, we are calling it "redditbot".
2. The allowed_domains is optional. We are setting access permissions for the crawler, limiting the domains it can crawl.
3. The parse function will be called every time a webpage is successfully crawled.

We have the update the start_urls argument in the class RedditbotSpider.

```
start_urls = ['https://www.reddit.com/r/gameofthrones/']
```

We corrected the URL so that it has the secured https argument. This is very important. If a website is secured, you will not be able to scrape data using the unsecured http URL. Here's the code block that you should paste instead of the default parse function definition:

```
def parse(self, response):
    #Extracting the content using css selectors
    title = response.css('h3._eYtD2XCVieq6emjKBH3m::text').extract()
    images_url = response.css("img::attr(src)").extract()
    #Pass the extracted content row wise
    for item in zip(titles,images_url):
    #create a dictionary to store the scraped info
    scraped_info = {
            'title' : item[0],
            'images_url': item[1],

    }

    #yield or give the scraped info to scrapy
    yield scraped_info
```

There are different ways to find required data. We are going to use the css class values of html to extract the text content and image URLs. We are extracting the title and featured image of all the threads on the Game of Thrones reddit homepage. With the extracted data, we create a dictionary and pass it to scrapy for processing with the yield statement. Since we have opted for CSS file output, the extracted data will be present in the folder we set in the settings.py.

After editing and saving the \myfirstspider\myfirstspider\spiders\redditbot.py file, you can start the crawler by going to the command prompt and running the following command:

```
scrapy crawl redditbot
```

Make sure you have changed the working directory in the command prompt to where you created the redditbot scraper. If you fail to change the directory, you will get a syntax error when you try to execute the command scrapy crawl redditbot.

You will see dozens of lines outputted on the command prompt as a result of the crawl command. It might look similar to this:

After the crawl is complete, you can go to the folder D:\Python27\myScripts\chapter 6\ourfirstscraper\ to read the scrapped content from the reddit.csv file. The csv file output might look like this:

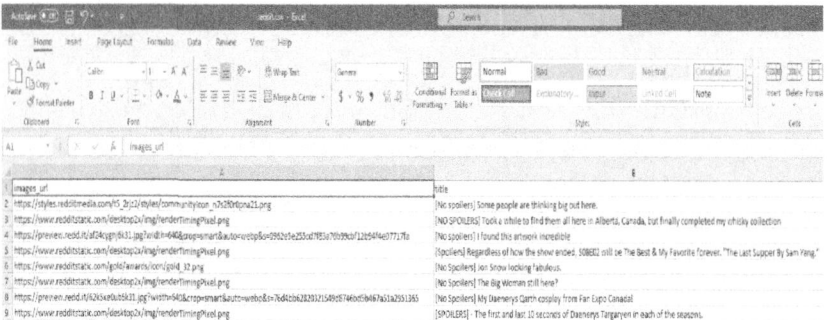

As you can see, we have the URLs of the images. The scrapy library also allows direct download of the images. For that, you need to add the following lines of code in the settings.py:

```
ITEM_PIPELINES = {
 'scrapy.pipelines.images.ImagesPipeline': 1
}
IMAGES_STORE = 'folder path where you want to download the images'
```

Make sure to remove or comment the CSV output lines if you want to download the images. Otherwise, the scraping might not work as expected.

You can further customize the spider to scrape large amount of different content. The biggest advantage of scrapy library is that it supports multithreading, so you can access multiple data points simultaneously. This is very helpful if you are scraping extremely large sites with tons of data.

There are other scraping libraries available on Python. One of them is Beautiful Soup, which is a lot simpler to work with than Scrapy. However, it's not suitable to work on large projects as it cannot access multiple content at the same time. Scraping one image from a website is a piece of cake, but to scrape 100 images, you'll need to access each image individually.

Manipulating Images

There is a reason why we were focusing on image scraping in the previous section. Python is very savvy with image processing, you see. For a common user, when we say image processing, it means resizing, cropping, rotating, or applying different color filters. Such tasks are quite easy to do with Python. But before we dive into action, we have to learn a few basic concepts.

Images are a 2D collection of pixels. Each pixel contains either the color value that should cover that area. An iPhone X camera in standard mode, for instance, takes a picture that has 4032 pixels in width and 3024 pixels in height. That's a lot of pixels stacked together. No matter how large an image is, it can be represented by a mathematical matrix. Furthermore, there are a number of mathematical operations that you can perform on a matrix. Armed with this knowledge, let's start working with image manipulation.

We need the pillow and numpy libraries, which are all included in PythonWin.

```
import os, sys
from PIL import Image
import numpy as np

pathname=os.path.dirname(sys.argv[0])
filepath = os.path.join(pathname,"test.jpg")

image = PIL.Image.open(filepath)
image.show()
```

The above code will open the test.jpg image in the default application on Windows. The image has a resolution of 4961 x 3594 and a size of 4.07MB. Let's resize the image to a smaller resolution. By the way, you can also check the image resolution on Python this way:

```
print image.size
Let's resize image to a square 300 x 300 size.
resized_image = image.resize((300,300))
resized_image.show()
```

Note how the width and height is given in a tuple. Here's the output.

As you can see the resized image doesn't have the aspect ratio of the original image. Let's create a solution for this problem.

```
basewidth = 300
wpercent = (basewidth/float(image.size[0]))
hsize = int((float(image.size[1])*float(wpercent)))
resized_image = image.resize((basewidth,hsize), Image.ANTIALIAS)
resized_image.show()
```

Here's the output:

We are using the width = 300 as our reference point and calculating the required height to keep the aspect ratio. The Image.ANTIALIAS is a filter that makes the image look not grainy upon a resize to a smaller size. Let's now see how we can crop the image.

```
resized_image = image.crop((2644,1540,3220,1856))
```

We supply a tuple of left, top, right and bottom coordinates again. The output looks like this:

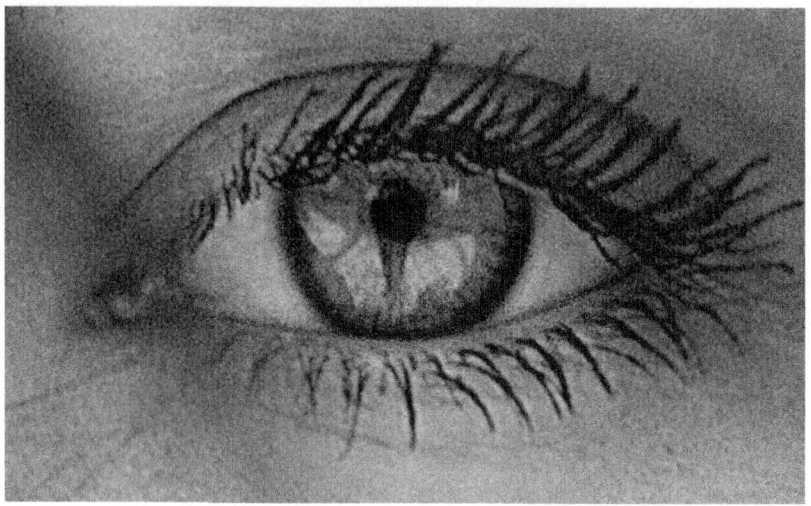

We can also do a mathematical trick that will help us crop the horizontally and vertically aligned central part of the image. Here's the code to do that:

```
width, height = image.size
left = width/4
top = height/4
right = 3 * width / 4
bottom = 3 * height / 4
resized_image = image.crop((top,left,right,bottom))
```

This is the output:

We can rotate the image by a single method.

```
resized_image = image.rotate(315)
```

Here's the output:

Remember when we said that an image is just a large matrix of pixels? We are going to use that idea to change colors of the image. Let's check the image for some information with the following command:

```
img_array = np.array(image)
print img_array.shape
```

The output for our image is:

```
(3594L, 4961L, 3L)
```

The first two numbers are the resolution of the image. The third number, 3L, denotes the color scheme of the image. To convert the image to grayscale, we just need to update the 3L to L. Here's the code and output for that:

```
resized_image = image.convert("L")
```

Let's convert the image to black and white. There are different algorithms available online that you can use for this, but we are going with the most simple solution. Specifically, we will take the grayscale image and use a value of 100 as our threshold. For all pixel values greater than 100, we are going to reset them to 255, while all other values will be rest to zero. Note that 255 means white and zero means black. Here's the code to do that:

```
threshold = 100
gray_image = image.convert("L")
img_array = np.array(gray_image)
for i in range(0, len(img_array)):
    for j in range(0, len(img_array[i])):
        if img_array[i][j] >= threshold:
            img_array[i][j] = 255
        else:
```

```
        img_array[i][j] = 0
bw_image = PIL.Image.fromarray(img_array)

bw_image.show()
```

Depending upon how large your image is, this process can take a while. Here's the output. Cool, right?

Automating Emails and Text Messages

Email Messages

To send emails with Python, we will need to sign up with an email service like Gmail. For testing purposes, we can create a local Simple Mail Transfer Protocol (SMTP) server but not use it to send emails.

To set up a Gmail account, go to gmail.com and sign up with an email ID. It is advisable to create a separate ID even if you have a Gmail account because we'll have to lower security level on this account for it to work with Python. (Read: It would be vulnerable to hacking.) During account setup, don't choose the two-step verification option. Once it is ready, go to Account Security settings and turn on the "Allow less secure apps" option.

With the Gmail account setup, we need to choose a Python library that'll be able to use that account to send emails. We are going to use the SMPT_SSL() module of the standard smtplib library to create a secure connection with Gmail and send an email. Here's the code that you need:

```
import smtplib, ssl

port = 465  # For SSL
smtp_server = "smtp.gmail.com"
password = input("Type your password and press enter: ")

# Create a secure SSL context
context = ssl.create_default_context()

# Email body
sender_email = "new_id@gmail.com" # gmail address you signed up
receiver_email = "xyz@gmail.com" # receiver's address
message = """\
Subject: Hi there

This message is sent from Python."""


with smtplib.SMTP_SSL(smtp_server, port, context=context) as server:
    server.login(sender_email, password)
    server.sendmail(sender_email, receiver_email, message)
```

This is a good example to send a plain text email.

Meanwhile, to send an html formatted email, we'll have to make use of standard mime libraries available in Python. Note that formatted html emails are sometimes blocked by email clients, so it's a good idea to combine plain text and html parts in one email. We are going to follow this practice in our example.

```
import smtplib, ssl
from email.mime.text import MIMEText
from email.mime.multipart import MIMEMultipart

port = 465  # For SSL
smtp_server = "smtp.gmail.com"
password = input("Type your password and press enter:")
```

```
sender_email = "new_id@gmail.com" # gmail address you signed up
receiver_email = "xyz@gmail.com" # receiver's address

message = MIMEMultipart("alternative")
message["Subject"] = "Testing multipart email sending"
message["From"] = sender_email
message["To"] = receiver_email

# Email body with plain text and formatted html parts
text = """\
Hi,
I hope you are doing well."""
html = """\
<html>
  <body>
      <p>Hi,<br>
      How are you?<br>
      I hope you are doing well!
      </p>
  </body>
</html>
"""

# Convert email body parts to MIME objects
part1 = MIMEText(text, "plain")
part2 = MIMEText(html, "html")

# Join MIME objects to create MIME message
message.attach(part1)
message.attach(part2)

# Create secure connection with server and send email
context = ssl.create_default_context()
with smtplib.SMTP_SSL(smtp_server, port, context=context) as server:
      server.login(sender_email, password)
      server.sendmail(
      sender_email, receiver_email, message.as_string()
      )
```

One last thing we are going to look at is how to send attachments. These are the extra lines that you'll have to add an attachment. In this example, we are sending a PDF file as an attachment.

```
# Open PDF file in binary mode
with open(filename, "rb") as attachment:
      # Add file as application/octet-stream
      part = MIMEBase("application", "octet-stream")
      part.set_payload(attachment.read())

# Encode file in ASCII characters to send by email
encoders.encode_base64(part)
```

```
# Add header as key/value pair to attachment part
part.add_header(
    "Content-Disposition",
    f"attachment; filename= {filename}",
)
# Add attachment to MIME message
message.attach(part)
```

This template can be further enhanced to send emails to multiple addresses. It is important to note that the free Gmail server in use has limits on sending and receiving emails over certain periods of time. It might be a good idea to use sleep() to create delays in sending emails. Also, Task Scheduling can be used to send a fixed amount of emails every day.

Text Messages

To send text messages, you'll need to get a third-party subscription to use their network gateway. Twilio is one of the most popular online services that can integrate with Python quickly. After getting a Twilio subscription and receiving the account ID and authorization token, we can start by installing the Twilio library in Python.

```
python -m pip install twilio
```

Sending a message is very easy, thanks to Twilio's awesome API. Here's a sample code:

```
from twilio.rest import Client

account_sid = 'ACXXXXXXXXXXXXXXXXXXXXXXXXXXXXXXXX'
auth_token = 'your_auth_token'
client = Client(account_sid, auth_token)

message = client.messages \
            .create(
            body="Hello, Universe!",
            from_='your_number',
            to='receiver_number'
            )

print(message.sid)
```

Change the account_sid and auth_token values from the values in your Twilio account. Also, alter the "from" number to the one bought from Twilio. Add the number you want to send the text to in the "to". Save the code with the name "send_sms.py". After executing the code, the message will be sent right away and delivered in a few minutes.

GUI Automation

We have already seen many GUI elements in previous chapters. Taking input and asking users for files and folders by selection has been a good practice. What if we can take control of the input devices and have them interact with GUI elements automatically? It can help us do trivial tasks, such as filling out forms or accepting ToS on websites.

We can use the external library pyautogui for this. On Windows, we will not need any other library, so let's install this particular library and start working with it.

```
python -m pip install pyautogui
```

Word of caution: Letting Python take control of the mouse and keyboard means you are forfeiting your control over them. In case your code is buggy, you might lose control indefinitely. Then, it'll be very hard to shut down the program execution due to not having any input. Even if your coding isn't faulty, Python can use the input devices faster than the application it's interacting with. It's very important to plan for contingencies in such situations. For instance, you can pull your desktop's power cord or perform hard shutdown on the laptop whenever you want, but the damage might already be done by then.

The good thing about pyautogui is that it has built-in pause and failsafe features. The failsafe is activated when the mouse moves to the upper-left corner of the screen. You can turn on the failsafe and set the pause value to number of seconds before you start working.

```
import pyautogui
pyautogui.FAILSAFE = True
pyautogui.PAUSE = 1
```

Now, let's see what's the current screen resolution is to know your playing field size.

```
pyautogui.size()
```

Once you have the screen size, you can start moving your mouse.

Mouse Automation

```
for i in range(10):
        pyautogui.moveTo(100, 100, duration=0.25)
        pyautogui.moveTo(200, 100, duration=0.25)
        pyautogui.moveTo(200, 200, duration=0.25)
        pyautogui.moveTo(100, 200, duration=0.25)
```

This will move the mouse in a square pattern in the clockwise direction. Each movement will happen in 0.25 seconds as set in the moveTo() method. In the above example, the pixel coordinates given are fixed. You can also move the mouse relative to its current position.

```
pyautogui.moveRel(100, 100, duration=0.25)
To get the current mouse position, use the following:
pyautogui.position()
Now, to have the mouse click, we can use the method click().
pyautogui.click(10, 5)
```

The coordinates provided to the click() method are real, not relative. This is a full click, which means pressing and releasing of the mouse button. You can use pyautogui.mouseDown() and pyautogui,mouseUp() for specific mouse button actions. The pyautogui.doubleClick() offers even more as it'll perform a double click with the left mouse button. You can automate a right click with pyautogui.rightClick() and a middle button click with pyautogui.middleClick().

To perform dragging, you can use pyautogui,dragTo() and pyautogui.dragRel(), which have similar functions to moveTo() and moveRel(). However, this time, the mouse button will remain clicked during the cursor movement. To automate the mousewheel to perform scrolling, there's the scroll() that takes an integer value as a unit of how much screen should move up (positive value) or down (negative value). The integer values will behave differently on different screen sizes and operating systems. Scrolling will begin from the current cursor location.

Furthermore, you can even take a screenshot with pyautogui.

```
img_screen = pyautogui.screenshot()
```

Keyboard Automation

The pyautogui.typewrite() can be used to virtually press keys on the keyboard. The result will depend on the application currently active. You can pass any string value to typewrite(), and it'll be typed in the current window by automating keypresses. We can add a delay so that every letter in the given string will be typed after a pause of specified duration.

```
pyautogui.typewrite("Hello, Universe!", 0.25)
```

To press keys that are not letter, such as Enter, there are special strings denoted that makes it easier to automate their keypress. For example, the Enter button has string "enter". Likewise, Escape key has "esc", and "right" is for Right Arrow key. Here's a table to show all the strings assigned to different keypresses.

Key String	Meaning
'a', 'b', 'c', 'A', 'B', 'C', '1', '2', '3', '!', '@', '#', and so on	keys for single characters
'enter' (or 'return'or '\n')	ENTER key
'esc'	ESC key
'shiftleft', 'shiftright'	Left and Right SHIFT keys
'altleft','altright'	Left and Right ALT keys
'ctrlleft','ctrlright'	Left and Right CTRL keys

'tab' or '\t'	TAB key
'backspace','delete'	BACKSPACE and DELETE keys
'pageup','pagedown'	PAGE UP and PAGE DOWN keys
'home','end'	HOME and END keys
'up','down','left','right'	ARROW keys
'f1','f2','f3' and so on...	F1 to F12 keys
'volumeup','volumedown','mute'	VOLUME control keys (Your keyboard might have these keys, but your system might still be able to recognize these commands.)
'pause'	PAUSE key
'capslock','numlock','scrolllock'	LOCK keys
'insert'	INSERT or INS key
'printscreen'	PRINT SCREEN or PRTSC key
'winleft','winright'	Left and Right WIN keys (Windows only)

We can also type special characters. The following code will have a dollar sign ($) typed on the screen automatically.

```
pyautogui.keyDown('shift')
pyautogui.press('4')
pyautogui.keyUp('shift')
```

To perform actions like "copy" (where you have to press CTRL and C keys together), you can have the following shortcut approach:

```
pyautogui.hotkey('ctrl','c')
```

Exercise

Create a Python script that scrapes one quote from http://quotes.toscrape.com/.

CONCLUSION

T hank you for finishing this book. It has been quite a journey. I hope you are now prepared to take on more challenging tasks with Python. The purpose of this book was to build the basics and spark the curiosity by giving you a glimpse into the strengths of Python.

Once you have developed good skills with Python 2.7, learning Python 3.0+ will be a breeze. There are not many changes, and Appendix B will help you get started on it.

REFERENCES

Downey, A. (2015). Think Python 2e [PDF File]. Retrieved from https://greenteapress.com/wp/think-python-2e/

Hammond, M. & Robinson, A. (2000). Python Programming on Win32: Help for Windows Programmers. Sebastopol, CA: O'Reilly & Associates, Inc.

Barry, P. (2016). Head First Python: A Brain-Friendly Guide. Sebastopol, CA: O'Reilly & Associates, Inc.

Sweigart, Al. (2015). Automate The Boring Stuff with Python: Practical Programming for Total Beginners. San Francisco, CA: No Starch Press, Inc.

Kanetkar, Y. & Kanetkar, A. (2019). Let Us Python: Python Is Future, Embrace it Fast. New Delhi, India: BPB Publications.

Althoff, C. (2017). The Self-Taught Programmer: The Definitive Guide to Programming Professionally. Los Altos, CA: Self-Taught Media.

Chan, J. (2014). Python: Learn Python in One Day and Learn It Well. Scotts Valley, CA: CreateSpace Independent Publishing Platform.

Kernighan, B. & Ritchie, D. (1979). The C Programming Language. Englewood Cliffs, NJ: Prentice Hall.

Bader, D. (2017). Python Tricks: A Buffet of Awesome Python Features. Vancouver, BC: Dan Bader.

Ramalho, L. (2014). Fluent Python: Clear, Concise, and Effective Programming. Sebastopol, CA: O'Reilly & Associates, Inc.
Beazley, D. & Jones, B. K. (2013). Python Cookbook. Sebastopol, CA: O'Reilly & Associates, Inc.

APPENDICES

Appendix A: Answers to Exercises

Chapter 1

A1. 01010100 01101000 01101001 01110011 00100000 01101001
01110011 00100000 01110100 01101000 01100101 00100000
01100010 01100101 01110011 01110100 00100000 01100010
01101111 01101111 01101011 00100000 01100101 01110110
01100101 01110010 00100001

A2. 54 68 69 73 20 69 73 20 74 68 65 20 62 65 73 74 20 62 6f 6f
6b 20 65 76 65 72 21

A3. Python was created in the year 1991.

A4. Niklaus Wirth developed Pascal.

A5. No, Python is a modern high-level language.

A6. Data was punched as a hole onto the card. The presence and
absence of a hole was interpreted by computers to read information
from a punch card.

A7. Perl was invented to process text files efficiently.

A8. Basic was designed by John G. Kemeny and Thomas E. Kurtz.

A9. The algorithm for the Bahamas vacation goes like this:

1. Start with financial planning.
2. Get extended leave approved from your work.
3. Research online for the vacation package that fits the budget and book it, but choose to pay later.
4. Call local travel agencies and haggle for better prices.
5. If you are successful in step 2, book with the local agency or finalize online booking payment.
6. Surprise the family with the vacation announcement.
7. Start the preparation by going shopping. Make sure not to go over budget.
8. Enjoy the vacation with your loved ones.

A10. Here is the flowchart for the Bahamas vacation:

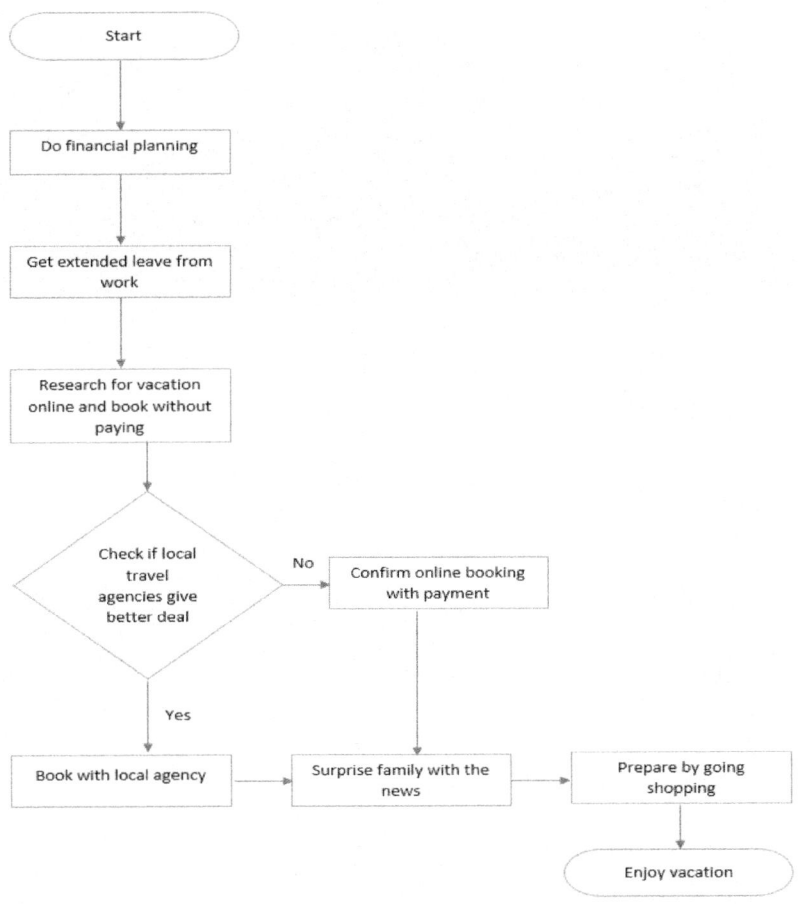

Chapter 2

A1. We are using Windows operating system based platform to learn Python in this book.

A2. We are using the most famous ActivePython 2.7 from ActiveState and getting extra benefits by adding Mark Hammond's (PythonWin) to it.

A3. Without Mark Hammond's contributions over the years, it would never have been possible for Python to thrive on Windows platform.

A4. ActiveState ActivePython, PyCharm, and PyPy

A5. Spyder, Thonny, and PyCharm

A6. Python's package manager is called pip.

A7. print "Hello, Universe!"

A8. print "Andrew Warner!"
Note: You should use your own name in place of Andrew Warner.

A9. Follow the instructions in Chapter 2 under the subheading "What Is a Module?" to create, save, and run a module. You can name the file as "my-name.py". There will only be a single line of code. (Note: You should use your own name in place of Andrew Warner.)

print "Andrew Warner!"

A10. By installing Mark Hammond's PythonWin, we have already setup the pywin32 package that provides useful tools to perform various tasks on Windows.

Chapter 3

A1.

```
urname = raw_input("Please enter your name: ")
for i in range(1,11):
    print "%d- %s" % (i, urname)
```

A2.

```
getstring = raw_input("Please enter a sentence: ")
space = " "
count = getstring.count(space)
print "Here is your sentence: "+getstring
print "The number of spaces in your given sentence is: %d" %
count
```

A3.

```
zipcoderange = {
    "AK" : ["99501-99950"],
    "AL" : ["35004-36925"],
    "AR" : ["71601-72959", "75502-75502"],
    "AZ" : ["85001-86556"],
    "CA" : ["90001-96162"],
    "CO" : ["80001-81658"],
    "CT" : ["6001-6389", "6401-6928"],
    "DC" : ["20001-20039", "20042-20599", "20799-20799"],
    "DE" : ["19701-19980"],
    "FL" : ["32004-34997"],
    "GA" : ["30001-31999", "39901-39901"],
    "HI" : ["96701-96898"],
    "IA" : ["50001-52809", "68119-68120"],
    "ID" : ["83201-83876"],
    "IL" : ["60001-62999"],
    "IN" : ["46001-47997"],
    "KS" : ["66002-67954"],
    "KY" : ["40003-42788"],
    "LA" : ["70001-71232", "71234-71497"],
    "MA" : ["1001-2791", "5501-5544"],
    "MD" : ["20331-20331", "20335-20797", "20812-21930"],
    "ME" : ["3901-4992"],
    "MI" : ["48001-49971"],
    "MN" : ["55001-56763"],
    "MO" : ["63001-65899"],
    "MS" : ["38601-39776"],
    "MS" : ["71233-71233"],
```

```
    "MT" : ["59001-59937"],
    "NC" : ["27006-28909"],
    "ND" : ["58001-58856"],
    "NE" : ["68001-68118", "68122-69367"],
    "NH" : ["3031-3897"],
    "NJ" : ["7001-8989"],
    "NM" : ["87001-88441"],
    "NV" : ["88901-89883"],
    "NY" : ["6390-6390", "10001-14975"],
    "OH" : ["43001-45999"],
    "OK" : ["73001-73199", "73401-74966"],
    "OR" : ["97001-97920"],
    "PA" : ["15001-19640"],
    "PR" : ["0-0"],
    "RI" : ["2801-2940"],
    "SC" : ["29001-29948"],
    "SD" : ["57001-57799"],
    "TN" : ["37010-38589"],
    "TX" : ["73301-73301", "75001-75501", "75503-79999",
"88510-88589"],
    "UT" : ["84001-84784"],
    "VA" : ["20040-20041", "20040-20167", "20042-20042",
"22001-24658"],
    "VT" : ["5001-5495", "5601-5907"],
    "WA" : ["98001-99403"],
    "WI" : ["53001-54990"],
    "WV" : ["24701-26886"],
    "WY" : ["82001-83128"]
}
userzip = raw_input("Please enter your state two digit code (ST):
")
userziprange = zipcoderange[userzip]
for i in userziprange:
    print "Zip range for %s state: %s" % (userzip , i)
```

A4.

```
    numstr1 = raw_input("Enter the range start number (lower limit):
")
```

```
numstr2 = raw_input("Enter the range end number (upper limit):
")
num1 = int(numstr1)
num2 = int(numstr2)

print "Between %s and %s, the prime numbers are: " % (numstr1,
numstr2)

for num in range(num1, num2+1):
    if num > 1:
        for i in range(2,num):
            if (num % i) == 0:
                break
        else:
            print num
```

A5.

```
list = []
for i in range(0,3):
    numstr = raw_input("Please enter a number: ")
    num = int(numstr)
    list.append(num)

print "The largest number you entered was:",max(list)
```

Chapter 4

A1. Operating system is a software that provides core functionality to a computer. It controls all the hardware parts and manages the resources real-time. It also executes the applications user wants to run on the computer. Windows, Mac OS, and Linux are a few famous operating systems.

A2. No, MS Office is not the only software suite with spreadsheet and word-processing applications. Google provides an online service that has Sheets and Docs as well.

A3. Oracle is a database management software developed by Oracle Corporation. It is a proprietary technology that is used by giant corporations to handle their data.

A4.
```
import os,sys

num = int(raw_input("Please enter a positive integer number: "))
multtable = []

for i in range(1,11):
    table_row = str(num)+" x "+str(i)+" = "+str(num*i)
    multtable.append(table_row)

a=os.path.dirname(sys.argv[0])
link=os.path.join(a,"multiplicationtable.txt")
text=open(link,'w')

text.write("Multiplication table of "+str(num)+'\n\n')
for item in multtable:
    text.write(item+'\n')

text.close()
```

A5.
```
import os

os.system('copy multiplicationtable.txt
C:\Users\andrew\Desktop\multiplicationtablecopy.txt')
```
A6.
```
import os,sys
import random

pathname=os.path.dirname(sys.argv[0])
textfiles=dict()

for name in os.listdir(pathname):
    path=os.path.join(pathname,name)
    if os.path.isfile(path):
        splitting=os.path.splitext(name)
        if splitting[1]==".txt":
            textfiles[splitting[0]]=None
```

```
for item in textfiles:
    randomnum = str(random.randint(1001,10000))
    src = os.path.join(pathname,item+".txt")
    dest = os.path.join(pathname,item+"_"+randomnum+".txt")
    #print dest
    os.rename(src, dest)
```

Chapter 5

A1.
```
from collections import OrderedDict

oDict = OrderedDict()
oDict['one'] = 1
oDict['two'] = 2
oDict['three'] = 3
oDict['four'] = 4

for key, value in oDict.items():
    print key, value
```

A2.
```
import os, sys
import win32com.client as win32
from collections import OrderedDict

userdata = OrderedDict()

data_headers = ['First Name', 'Last Name', 'Age', 'Zip',
'Education', 'Driver Status? (Yes/No)', 'Height', 'Weight', 'Avg Time
Spent on Cell Phone Daily', 'Commute Time to Work']

for i in data_headers:
    userdata[i] = raw_input("Please Enter Your "+i+":")



#write the data to an excel file
excel = win32.Dispatch("Excel.Application")
```

```
excel.Visible = True
wb = excel.Workbooks.Add()

ws = wb.Sheets.Add()
ws.Name = "Python Created"

#single loop, writing a column
for i in range(0, len(data_headers)):
    j = i + 1
    ws.Cells(1,j).Value = data_headers[i]
    ws.Cells(2,j).Value = userdata[data_headers[i]]

pathname=os.path.dirname(sys.argv[0])
filepath=os.path.join(pathname,"populatedexcelfile.xlsx")
wb.SaveAs(filepath)
wb.Close()
excel.Application.Quit()
```

A3.
```
import os, sys, time
import win32com.client as win32

pathname=os.path.dirname(sys.argv[0])
excel=win32.gencache.EnsureDispatch('Excel.Application')
excel.Visible = True

filepath=os.path.join(pathname,"populatedexcelfile.xlsx")
wb=excel.Workbooks.Open(filepath)
ws=wb.Worksheets('Sheet1')
ws.Name = "Extra Sheet"
wb.SaveAs(filepath)
wb.Close()
excel.Application.Quit()
```

A4.
```
import os, sys
import win32com.client as win32

#write the data to an excel file
```

```
excel = win32.Dispatch("Excel.Application")
excel.Visible = True
wb=excel.Workbooks.Open(filepath)

ws=wb.Worksheets('Python Created')
wsnew=wb.Worksheets('Extra Sheet')

j = 10
for i in range(1,11):
wsnew.Cells(1,i).Value = ws.Cells(1,j).Value
wsnew.Cells(2,i).Value = ws.Cells(2,j).Value
j = j - 1
```

A5.
```
root = Tkinter.Tk()
root.withdraw() #use to hide tkinter window
file                                          =
tkFileDialog.asksaveasfilename(parent=root,initialdir="/",filetypes =
(("Excel file","*.xlsx"),("Excel old file","*.xls")))
filepathnew = file.replace("/","\\")
wb.SaveAs(filepathnew)
wb.Close()
excel.Application.Quit()
```

A6.
```
import os, sys
import win32com.client as win32

excel = win32.Dispatch("Excel.Application")
excel.Visible = True
wb=excel.Workbooks.Add()

ws=wb.Worksheets('Sheet1')
ws.Name = "Python Created"
```

```
ws.Cells(1,1).Value = "List of prime numbers between 0 and 10000"
j = 2
for num in range(0, 10000+1):
   if num > 1:
      for i in range(2,num):
         if (num % i) == 0:
            break
      else:
         ws.Cells(j,1).Value = num
         j = j + 1


pathname=os.path.dirname(sys.argv[0])
filepath=os.path.join(pathname,"primenumberexcelfile.xls")
wb.SaveAs(filepath)
wb.Close()
excel.Application.Quit()
```

A7.
```
import PyPDF2
import os, sys


pathname = os.path.dirname(sys.argv[0])
filepath = os.path.join(pathname,"sample.pdf")
pdffile = open(filepath,'rb')
readpdf = PyPDF2.PdfFileReader(pdffile)
pagenum = readpdf.numPages

for i in range(pagenum):
   pdfpage = readpdf.getPage(i)
   print "Page #",i+1
   print pdfpage.extractText()
```

A8.
```
import PyPDF2
```

```python
import os, sys
import win32com.client as win32

pathname = os.path.dirname(sys.argv[0])
filepath = os.path.join(pathname,"sample.pdf")
pdfdata = []

pdffile = open(filepath,'rb')
readpdf = PyPDF2.PdfFileReader(pdffile)
pagenum = readpdf.numPages

word = win32.gencache.EnsureDispatch('Word.Application')
doc = word.Documents.Add()
word.Visible = True

for i in range(pagenum):
    pdfpage = readpdf.getPage(i)
    print "Page #",i+1
    pdfdata.append(pdfpage.extractText())

rng = doc.Range(0,0)

for dataread in pdfdata:
    str = dataread+"\r"
    rng.InsertAfter(str)

pathname=os.path.dirname(sys.argv[0])
filepath=os.path.join(pathname,"readsamplepdf.docx")
doc.SaveAs(filepath)
word.Application.Quit()

A9.
import csv
import os, sys
```

```
pathname=os.path.dirname(sys.argv[0])
filepath = os.path.join(pathname,"largest_number.csv")


with open(filepath, mode='w') as csv_file:
    fieldnames = ['Number 1', 'Number 2', 'Number 3', 'Number 4',
'Number 5', 'Number 6', 'Number 7', 'Number 8', 'Number 9',
'Number 10', 'Number 11', 'Number 12', 'Number 13', 'Number 14',
'Number 15', 'Number 16', 'Number 17', 'Number 18', 'Number 19',
'Number 20']
    datadict = {}
    for i in range (1,21):
        strrrr = "Number "+str(i)
        datadict[strrrr] = int(raw_input("Please enter a number: "))
    writer = csv.DictWriter(csv_file, fieldnames=fieldnames)

    writer.writeheader()
    writer.writerow(datadict)

dataset = []
with open(filepath, mode='r') as csv_file:
    csv_reader = csv.DictReader(csv_file)
    for row in csv_reader:
        for i in row.values():
            dataset.append(int(i))

    print max(dataset)
    A10.
    import json
    jsondata = json.dumps(max(dataset))
```

Chapter 6

A1. Here's the crawler code.

```
# -*- coding: utf-8 -*-
import scrapy


class QuotescraperSpider(scrapy.Spider):
    name = 'quotescraper'
    allowed_domains = ['quotes.toscrape.com']
    start_urls = ['http://quotes.toscrape.com/']

    def parse(self, response):
        quotes = response.css(".quote .text::text").extract()
        author = response.css(".quote .author::text").extract()

        for item in zip(quotes,author):
            scraped_info = {
                "quotes":item[0],
                "author":item[1],
                }
            yield scraped_info
```

Appendix B: Differences in Python 3.x

Print Statement

In Python 2.7, the print statement looks like this:
print "Hello, Universe!"
In Python 3.0+, the print statement must be similar to the one below. Yes, it looks more like C and also supports many similar operators.
print("Hello, Universe!")
Actually, Python 2.7 also supports parentheses but only as an option.

Input Statement

There's no raw_input() in Python 3.0+. It has been discarded and input() has been reinvented to support all input functionalities.
input("Please enter your name: ")
Future Module
You can make your Python 2.7 code to run in Python 3.0+ by using the future() module.
from future import print

Integer Division

In Python 2.7, integers divided by integers will always result in an integer.

```
>>> 3/2
1
```

Dividing integer with integer might return a float in Python 3.0+, though.

```
>>> 3/2
1.5
```

Unicode

Python 2.7 supports ASCII, str(), and unicode(), but there was no byte type.
In Python 3.0+, there are two byte classes, as well as Unicode (UTF-8) string.

Xrange

In Python 2.7, xrange() was popularly used in for loops that only had one-time iterations. It was faster, but in situations where iterations had to be repeated multiple times, range() was better.

In Python 3, there's no xrange(). Instead, range() has the benefits of xrange().

Comparing Unordered Types

Comparing unordered types shouldn't have been allowed. In Python 2.7, it would have returned false, which was incorrect. This has been fixed in Python 3.0+.

Dictionary Ordering

In Python 2.7, dictionary key-pairs are randomly stored. To create an ordered dictionary in Python 2.7, we have to use the OrderedDict() module.

In Python 3.0+, the key-pair order will remain in the same order as they are added to the dictionary.

Values Inside For Loop Don't Leak

In Python 2.7, if you use a variable as iterator, its previous value will be overwritten.

```
i = 2
for i in range(100,200):
    pass

print i
```

This would result in 199 as output. In Python 3.0+, however, it would result in an output of 2.

There are more differences between Python 2.7 and Python 3.0. Take your time in learning the changes and make the switch when you feel comfortable

Finally, I want to thank you the reader, for coming along on this ride. I hope you had as much fun as I did. If so, please take a moment to post a review and tell a friend.

Feel free to contact me if you have any questions.
I wish you the best of luck.

Andrew Warner.

Printed in Great Britain
by Amazon